CONTEMPORARY PHILOSOPHICAL ALTERNATIVES
AND THE CRISIS OF THE TRUTH

CONTEMPORARY PHILOSOPHICAL ALTERNATIVES AND THE CRISIS OF TRUTH

A CRITICAL STUDY OF POSITIVISM, EXISTENTIALISM
AND MARXISM

by

G. A. RAUCHE

University College of Durban

MARTINUS NIJHOFF / THE HAGUE / 1970

ISBN 90 247 5017 2

PRINTED IN THE NETHERLANDS

LIST OF CONTENTS

INTRODUCTION

The function of philosophy may be circumscribed as consisting in making a keen analysis of the peculiar nature of the crisis-situation, as it has existed among men throughout the centuries of human history, and as it manifested itself in definite ways at the various stages of this history. That is to say, philosophy may be regarded as the discipline which, again and again, will have to determine the authenticity of man's existence in the light of the changing conditions of life, i.e., man's changing needs and interests. Fundamentally, these needs may be regarded as being of a material, an intellectual, an aesthetical and a spiritual kind. On the grounds of the crisis, which inevitably exists among men on account of the controversial nature of their various truth-perspectives, as they are postulated on a personal level, in the sciences, in history, in the fine arts and in theology, man creates and re-creates the goods of civilization and the cultural values. The task of philosophy consists then in making an ever new assessment of man's changing needs, interests and aspirations on the basis of the specific conflicts and problems with which man wrestles at a certain historical stage. It is in this way that the important philosophical systems were constructed, which we still admire to-day. It is on this account that new philosophical concepts were formed and that a re-assessment of the basic human values, notably ethical ones, took place. Acting in this manner, philosophy was able to determine the authenticity of man's existence, as an existence that was in line with the call of the times, or the *Zeitgeist*. Philosophy may thus be called an open science, which finds it impossible to give a conclusive answer to its permanent question about truth. This is so because any answer it gives to this basic question on the part of man is only a truth-perspective, which is developed under particular historical circumstances and in the particular existential situation in which man happens to find himself at the time. The answer is always given in reaction to some other philosophical project, which is already in existence and which the new system somehow calls in question, thereby entering into a controversial relation with it, and, in so doing, developing a truth-perspective in its own turn, which often takes man a step further. It is by the constant change of the situation as a result of the formulation of ever new philosophical alternatives for coping with the constant crisis of truth that ever new dimensions of truth are discovered by man and that the process of human thinking unfolds as a continual historical process. It is thus impossible to conceive philosophy as a homogeneous science with only one method. It is a science of many methods and approaches, one rising out of the other in its permanent quest for truth, which it has to keep up in the light of the permanent crisis of truth. This crisis occurs as a result of the questionable character of its methodologically constituted truth-perspectives or alternatives for coping with the crisis of truth.

Since these truth-perspectives, at the same time, represent man's self-projection into the world from the particular situation in which he finds himself, it follows that these alternatives for coping with the crisis of truth are of existential significance. Through them, man takes possession of the world in a rational manner and arranges his surroundings in a rational way. And if his particular philosophical project is called in question by someone else, his existence is undermined. He feels insecure and fears the collapse of his rationally constituted universe. This explains the tenacity and obduracy with which philosophers have clung to their systems and have defended them against all criticism and attack. But in spite of this, life went on. By their claim to totality and universality, the philosophers concerned invited their own downfall. The very rational character of the philosophical systems concerned, their very methodological nature, pointed beyond themselves, in that they opened the way for other means of rationalizing the world. And every time the world was reorganized, the authentic nature of man's existence was redetermined in connection with the moral values that were implicit in the new system or approach. It was by the inevitable controversial relation that obtained among philosophical systems and the permanent crisis of human truth that philosophy, in a continual historical process, yielded ever new concepts and approaches, thus reorganizing the world in an ever new fashion and, in so doing, creating ever new problems and changing the situation. This in turn forced man to repeat the question about truth, the nature of the universe, the meaning and purpose of life and the authentic nature of human existence.

We can also formulate it in this way: Man asked a total question to which, on account of his finiteness and limitation, he could give only a limited answer.

It is this state of affairs that renders philosophy finite, contingent and existential. The existential circle works like this: Driven by a basic need for certainty and security, man asks the question about truth. The answer to this question creates fresh problems and conflicts, which again he seeks to overcome. It is this interplay between universal question and finite answer that keeps him going. It would be like the work of Sisyphus, except that it seems that the whole process is not meaningless; for it appears as though this is the way in which man seems to realize himself as a creative being of culture and civilization. Also, he has thereby improved his methodological and functional skill and has progressively civilized the world. The question is, however, how much has man gained and how much has he lost? We hope that the answer to this question will emerge in the course of our discussion of the process of human thinking as it occurs in philosophy. One thing is certain, however, if we wish to understand the nature of man, we must turn to philosophy. Through it, man's existential struggle becomes manifest in its manifold aspects. But to gain this understanding, we must not become preoccupied with one or two philosophical approaches in isolation from their historical foundation. If we wish to understand man's true nature, we must look at the philosophical alternatives for coping with the crisis of truth in their historical succession and in the light of the historical circumstances under which they were conceived. We must realize that the crisis of truth, as it is experienced by man, is an existential crisis, which has compelled him to project himself into the world in an ever new manner. It is in this way that man's thinking has unfolded and ever new dimensions of truth have been discovered, none of which stands isolated but every one of which is linked to another one in controversy and contradiction. In this way, one perspective of truth, as it were, stands on the shoulder of the other, so that, in spite of their controversial relationship, human thinking is one irreversible process, which must be seen in its continuity and entirety.

In this connection, a few outstanding examples will shed more light on what has been said: Plato may be said to have been confronted with the task of determining the authenticity of human existence in the face of the prevailing conflict of his time, namely, that between democratic and aristocratic thinking. This conflict split the inhabitants of the Athenian *polis* into two groups. Plato may be said to have solved the task of overcoming this conflict by the conception of a new social order and a new state under the *principle of identity*. This means that the ethical order of the cosmos, i.e., its rationality, reality, beauty and justice, as it emerges from the harmony of the opposites in the world thus pointing to its goodness, is reflected in the human soul. Leading an authentic existence, therefore, means, for Plato, building a society and a state in conformity with the structure of the human soul and, for this reason, also with that of the cosmos. The balance that is kept among the three social classes, the productive class of the merchants and agriculturists, the defending class of the warriors (*phylakes*) and the ruling class (*archontes*) corresponds to the balance that should be kept among the three parts of the human soul. These parts correspond to the three social classes and should each be governed by its respective virtue. The part that consists of the natural appetites of the soul should be ruled by the virtue of *sophrosyne* or self-control; the part that is designated by the noble affects of the soul should be dominated by the virtue of *andreia* or fortitude, strength of mind and of body; the rational part of the soul should be determined by the virtue of *sophia* or wisdom. If reason rules and keeps these parts in balance, then perfect harmony is achieved and *dikaiosyne* prevails.

By the principle of identity, therefore, i.e., if the structure of the soul and that of society correspond to the structure of the cosmos, truth as the highest good has been realized. In this event, man's needs are satisfied in that they have been brought into line with the different natural capacities of different men. In this way, all men are able to lead an authentic existence, i.e., an existence in conformity with their natural capacity and thus with their true nature.

By linking up with Plato, Aristotle postulates an alternative to Plato's attempt to overcome the basic conflict of his age. In order to cope with the existing corruption and injustice in the *polis* of his time, and in order to coordinate the interests of the citizens as far as this was possible and to meet their needs, Aristotle entered into controversy with Plato and conceived an alternative that called in question the system of Plato. In conformity with his more realistic world-view, namely, that the universal was to be found in the particular itself (instead of existing in a transcendent world of forms, as was held by Plato) and came into existence by the process of the actualization of matter as potential form, Aristotle based his ethics on the realization of man's rational self. For this reason he included in his ethics that which

Plato had tried to overcome by the stratification of society, namely, the senses. The realization of man's rational nature, therefore, meant the observance of the *golden mean* by *sophrosyne* or self-control. If everyone acted in this manner, husband and wife, brother and sister, citizens of the *polis*, *eudaimonia*, i.e., happiness would be achieved, and this achievement would have been made by rational insight into one's true nature and natural capacity. Aristotle's state, too, like that of Plato, had an educational function to perform and possessed a distinct moral character. The difference was that, with Aristotle, the leading of an authentic existence did not mean the pursuit of truth for the sake of truth, as it did with Plato, but it meant the striving for *eudaimonia* through the reasonable act, i.e., practising moderation or temperance (practical virtues) in wisdom or prudence (dianoetic virtues).

By virtue of this broad aim, Aristotle was able to contrast with one another several 'good' forms of state with several 'bad' ones. Patriarchal monarchy, responsible aristocracy, moderate democracy based on the communal sense of the brotherhood of its citizens, all of whom subordinated their individual private interests to the interests of the community, were judged to be good. Tyranny, as the selfish rule of one man, oligarchy, as the rule of the wealthy and their selfish interests, and ochlocracy, as the rule of the mob, were held to be bad.

If we pursue the course of the history of philosophy any further, we shall find that, after the collapse of the Greek *polis* and the inevitable failure of Greek philosophy to comprehend *the* truth (*arche*, first principle, first cause)[1] through man's own rational effort, a re-interpretation of basic values and the development of new concepts became imperative. Roughly speaking, this was at first done by Alexandrian philosophy in the face of great turmoil and upheaval. In those tempestuous times of growing unrest, uncertainty and anxiety, when empires fell and new ones came into existence, the need for certainty and the desire for happiness were raising the question again as to the authenticity of man's existence. Especially the problem of the nature of death assumed great importance.[2] Already the Stoics, Epicureans and the Sceptics battled with these problems. Neo-Platonism and Gnosticism made an attempt to determine man's destiny by clothing Eastern ideas in a

---

[1] This failure becomes apparent from the contradictory answers that were given by Greek philosophy to the question of truth.

[2] This problem became very acute again in our contemporary crisis. Especially the German poet-philosopher Rainer Maria Rilke and the philosopher Martin Heidegger are preoccupied with this problem. Sometimes the answers that are given to this problem by them bear much resemblance to the answers that were given to it earlier, especially by the Stoics.

Greek methodological form. In the West, however, it was the new Christian concept of faith that finally proved victorious in the fierce battle of philosophical and religious views that was raging within the Roman Empire. Faith had the advantage over reason in that it offered absolute certainty to the believer, and, in addition, led him to the experience of highest bliss and beatitude. Thus, eventually, the relation between reason and faith came to be investigated by Christian thinkers, and in the course of this investigation the theocentric scholastic method was developed with the help of Greek philosophy. The authenticity of man's existence was derived from God as the greatest good, no matter whether God was seen as highest wisdom (Thomas Aquinas) or as absolute will (Duns Scotus and William Occam). In the interest of the Oneness of truth (i.e., the unity of reason and faith), which was called in question by the penetration into western thinking of Averroistic ideas in the 13th century (Siger of Brabant), a Christian cosmos came to be built, notably by Albertus Magnus, Thomas Aquinas and Bonaventura. This cosmos comprised reason and faith in one. Its hierarchical structure (the realm of faith, reason and sensual experience) was reflected in the feudal structure of medieval society (clergy and nobility, bourgeoisie and peasants).

This whole outlook was changed again by the rising of the middle-class as a result of new discoveries and new inventions and the growth and increasing wealth and prosperity of the towns that followed in their wake. The middle class was by nature the negation of feudalist society. It is thus only natural that the middle class posited its truth in accordance with its specific needs and interests as they arose from its particular existential situation. It is not surprising, therefore, that the conflict between reason and faith, philosophy and theology, knowledge and belief, which scholastic thought sought to bridge by the subordination of reason to faith, was eventually resolved in favour of reason, philosophy and knowledge. For it was this that would promote the interests of the new historical class, the "bourgeoisie."

As a result of all this bustling human activity in the 14th and the 15th centuries, by which the horizons of his knowledge were considerably widened and his insight into nature and into himself was considerably increased, man, at first, shifted his interest towards himself. His curiosity about the ancient classical thinkers and writers was aroused again, and he began to read and to see them in the light of his own situation. In Renaissance thought, therefore, the theocentricity of medieval scholasticism was gradually superseded by an anthropocentric outlook. It is this anthropocentric approach to life and to the universe that is usually meant, when mention is made of the *humanism* of the period. This humanism is shown in painting, architecture and in Renaissance writing. In contrast to the theocentric outlook of medieval scholasticism, Renaissance thought finds the greatest good in man's personality. Man feels himself the centre of the universe. The universe is reflected in him, and he becomes the microcosm of the macrocosm. By the endless progression of his thinking, as it becomes manifest, for instance, through his power of endless integration and infinitesimal division (Nicolaus Cusanus) and by the metaphysical power of his feeling and his intuition, man is able to project himself into the infinite and to fuse with the universe.

The growing economic and political power of the middle class, however, caused philosophy to become more rational and more sober. In its quest for truth and knowledge and by the controversy as to the best method of acquiring knowledge, it exchanged the aesthetical approach of the Renaissance period for an empirical approach on the one hand and a rational method on the other. The empiricist Francis Bacon becomes the prophet of the inductive method on the one hand, René Descartes, the rationalist, becomes the advocate of the deductive method on the other. By the conception of the inductive and deductive methods in regard to knowledge, philosophy now presented alternatives that were more suitable to overcome the decadent scholasticism of a dying feudal society and that planted philosophy on firmer premises than did the somewhat blurred anthropological metaphysics of Renaissance thougt.

In what way, now, is human action determined by these two approaches as either good or evil? That this question is tantamount to the question of the authenticity of human existence need hardly be stressed. In the case of the rationalist alternative, especially the approach of Descartes, it is reason in the sense of the compelling necessity and clarity of the analytical judgment that is regarded as the highest good and in terms of which human action is judged. In other words, moral action issues from the self-evident character of our innate moral ideas and principles, which determine the authenticity of man's existence as one in reason. In the case of the empirical approach, it is the experience of pleasure and pain that by abstraction becomes the moral principle and the touchstone for *greater happiness*. To achieve this greatest good is, according to Locke, man's chief-concern in this world. It can only be achieved through rational insight. In directing his will towards this aim and for this purpose subordinating his will to reason, man becomes free and lives an authentic life, i.e., a life in agreement with his rational desire. The moral act is based on self-control, that is to say, action should not follow upon impulse, but only after reflection on its consequences for the community and thus for oneself. It is this government of our passions by our reason in the interests of the common good and thus to our own advantage which Locke means when he talks about the rational standstill of the will, i.e., the suspension of our desires. "But the forbearance of a too hasty compliance with our desires, the moderation and restraint of our passions, so that our understandings may be free to examine, and reason unbiassed gives its judgment, being that whereon a right direction of our conduct to true happiness depends; it is in this we should employ our chief care and endeavours."[3] According to Locke, greater happiness can be achieved only by reasonable action in the above sense. It is obvious that, for Locke, reasonable action is at the same time moral action, by which man experiences greater pleasure than the fleeting pleasure he experiences in the mere gratification of his passions, a gratification which results only in new uneasiness and desire.

It is the conception of greater happiness as the greatest good that has been conducive to the development of definite values in the new middle-class society, values which are still largely accepted by western society to-day. There is no doubt that Locke's pragmatic and liberal ethics has largely determined the norms and standards of conduct of western society up to the present time. In accordance with Locke's liberalism and individualism, it was the main function of the state to protect the right of every citizen to strive for greater happiness. Liberty thus meant the full enjoyment of this right by every citizen, who was to be free from oppression, violence and fear, when exercising this right. The advantage of such an ethics for a society that lives by trade and industrial enterprise is obvious.

In Germany, where the middle class had not yet developed to the same extent as it had developed in England and in France and where it was much more dependent on the authority of the state, philosophy interpreted freedom not as the rational striving for greater happiness, but as the overcoming of material interests and the material world by man on the strength of his rational autonomy. By treating nature as something inferior, from which the mind must free itself, philosophy treated man's material needs as unimportant.

In Kant's transcendentalism and Fichte's idealism the autonomy of

[3] John Locke, *On Human Understanding*, B. 2, XXI, 53.

man's mind or of man's reason is emphasized. Man's reason is placed in opposition to nature, it is essentially different from it. In following his reason, he ceases to be the slave of his material desires; he becomes free and is so able to lead an authentic existence. By making himself autonomous in this manner, he becomes a person. In other words, by subordinating his will to his reason, man can overcome the material world and his material appetites if he so wills. It is in this rational *ought* that Kant's and also Fichte's *categorical imperative* consists. Thou canst, therefore thou should'st. If this command is obeyed, then man's will is, so to speak, formalized. It receives a rational content, so that man will act in such a way that his action conforms to a universal moral principle. This ethics of duty, which culminates in the formula: duty for the sake of duty, becomes the code of conduct of Prussian officialdom, and by a special branch of it, the teachers, was inculcated in the nation. This idealistic ethics was also embraced by the English writer Thomas Carlyle.

The *raison d'être* of the Prussian state and Prussian society, as they existed in the 19th century, was derived from Hegel's concept of the *absolute spirit*. Hegel's conception of history as the objective externalization of this spirit suited the character of the Prussian state as a Christian monarchy very well. By the historical movement of the spirit the historical function of the then existing Prussian state and society became clear. This spirit is conceived as a dynamic principle of reason, which externalizes itself in nature and in history and so becomes objective. By a dialectical process, which is comprehended by the antithetical character of concepts, the spirit gradually liberates itself from its captivity in the world and returns to itself in perfect purity. As the pure concept, which comprehends all finite, antithetical concepts, it stands in an antithetical relationship with the world. Eastern, ancient-classical, medieval and modern Christian culture are but various stages in the process of the spirit's returning to itself. They represent the growing state of freedom of the spirit. Naturally, this process of the spirit's self-emancipation is regarded by Hegel as being completed in his own time. There the cycle of history is closed, philosophy has fulfilled itself and has become one with theology. Thus reason has become indentical with religion, knowledge with faith. The state as an expression of the general will (as this will manifests itself in the indivudual's rational striving) unites all citizens under the spirit as the most perfect, the most real, the most beautiful and the most holy. The state is an *ethical idea*, which man conceives as an immanent truth and which causes him to accept the state as his own. By identifying himself with the state, man leads an authentic existence. The affirmation of the state is a reasonable act because it brings man into line with reality (history). It is a moral act, which frees man from his selfishness and egoism; and last, but not least, it is a religious act, for thereby tribute is paid to the spirit. "Der Staat ist göttlicher Wille, als gegenwärtiger, sich zur wirklichen Gestalt und Organisation einer Welt entfaltender Geist," says Hegel.

Marx now claims that, by this act of man's self-creation in the spirit, Hegel has caused man to project himself into the clouds. By his doctrine of the spirit, with which man blends by the rational comprehension of its dialectical movement, so that it becomes an immanent truth, Hegel has avoided the real issues and conflicts of the time. He has "solved" them only in theory but not in practice, says Marx. This kind of "solution" of the current conflicts and problems of the age is deemed by Marx to serve only the needs and interests of the ruling social classes but not of the whole community. It is against the needs and interests of the new working class, which has come into existence as a result of rapid industrialization and which is fast becoming the major part of the population. By its total character and extreme idealism, Hegel's philosophy has estranged itself from reality. It so points beyond itself and thereby to its own negation. It is true, Marx concedes, that, by his dialectical method Hegel has shown that man creates himself by his rational activity, but such creation must not be one in spirit, but one in reality. It must not be one in theory, but one in practice. Human consciousness must not reflect the abstract idea, but concrete reality. What is most important to Marx is that, in creating himself, man must, by his productive activity, actually change the world in accordance with his true needs and interests. "The philosophers have only *interpreted* the world in different ways, what is important is to *change* it" exclaims Marx in his famous theses on Feuerbach.[4] The productive class, and therefore the one that is apt to change the world, is the working class, while the ruling or possessing class is naturally interested in the *status quo*. In order to perform their natural function of changing the world in a manner that the authenticity of man's (the labourer's) existence is realized, the members of the productive class must be freed from their self-estrangement and the unauthentic manner of their existence. Their

---

[4] This is a translation from German: „Die Philosophen haben die Welt nur verschieden *interpretiert*, es kömmt darauf an, sie zu *verändern*", in: *Karl Marx, Ausgewählte Schriften*, ed. by B. Goldenberg, p. 317. This is the 11th thesis and the last one of Marx's „Thesen über Feuerbach".

dehumanization is due to the fact that they have to sell themselves or their working capacity as a commodity and in competition with their colleagues to an exploiting class, which is in possession of the means of production and reaps the profits therefrom. In order to heal the rift in society and to harmonize the needs and interests of the productive class with those of society, the means of production must be controlled by the productive class itself. By taking over the means of production and by distributing the products in accordance with their natural needs, the members of the productive class become full men. By acting responsibly, i.e., in the general interest, they become free and are now able to lead an authentic existence.

Already in his doctoral disseration of 1841 entitled *Differenz der demokratischen und epikureischen Naturphilosophie*, but more so in his later works, Marx observed that, with Hegel, philosophy had become total and that, for this reason, the total break with it was inevitable, if man was to move from unauthentic to authentic existence. According to Marx, two totalities faced one another: a philosophy having become total itself and the real world of non-philosophy. Thus the having-become-philosophical of the world (with Hegel) demands an equally complete becoming-worldly of philosophy. In his dissertation Marx still shared the idealist standpoint of the young Hegelians, although he deviates from them by regarding philosophy as an ideal weapon of the revolutionary struggle against despotism. In the further development of his thought, Marx drew the conclusion that philosophy must merge with economics, not in the sense of economic theory, but in the sense of actual economy, which means it must merge with man's productive activity in the material sense of the word, by which the world is changed. Philosophy must become politics, not in the sense of mere political theory, but in the sense of actually bringing about the qualitative change in society that would meet the needs and interests of the labouring class, and thus of humanity. By the fusion of philosophy with economics and politics in the above sense, man would at the same time free himself from the thrall of religion. To this illusion man subscribes, as long as he is estranged from himself by the capitalist method of production. By being deprived of the possibility of improving his miserable position on account of the inevitable clash between private and general interest, he seeks to find compensation for the frustation of his needs in a dream world. Marx, therefore, concedes the need of religion as long as these conditions prevail. The moment, however, philosophy merges with economics and politics and thus becomes a weapon in the hands of the proletarian in order to effect the qualitative change of the social structure, man becomes independent of religion and self-reliant. Instead of trusting in God, he now puts all the confidence in himself.

Marx holds that, as historical materialism, philosophy must show that, on account of man's incessant productivity, which places man in a dialectical relationship with nature, history constitutes a dialectical process. From the slave-holder society, it moves to the feudal society of the middle ages, which changes into the capitalist form of society, which in turn will inevitably give birth to socialism. The latter is the transition stage between capitalism and communism and will be marked by the dictatorship of the proletariat. This dictatorship will cease when communism is fully realized. Thus by the dialectical relation between theory and practice, consciousness and matter, thinking and being, the subject and the object, man's material, intellectual, aesthetical and spiritual needs are realized. For as the productive process aims at the gratification of his material needs, it requires planning and theorizing; it makes man become conscious of his creative power and allows him to enjoy his creations; it also makes him develop faith in himself and in progress. Labour may thus be said to be regarded as the greatest good in Marx's philosophy. It is through labour that man determines the authenticity of his existence as a productive and, in this sense, an economic being. In conformity with the modern form of labour as it manifests itself in the modern mechanical and technological way of production, man comes to regard the communist structure of society as the only congenial form. Labour as the bridge between subject and object eventually resolves all conflict and contradiction that still exist between man and his surroundings and between man and man. Labour, in Marx's philosophy, may be said to be of logical, epistemological, metaphysical, aesthetical and ethical significance.

As a result of the rapid development of science and industry in the 19th century and the problems and conflicts that arose in connection with it, philosophy offered alternatives for coping with these problems that either more or less conformed with the scientific and technological methods, or that opposed them. Linking up with the most important philosophical approaches that were developed mostly in conformity with the change from the middle ages to the modern scientific and industrial era, namely, the rationalist-empiricist approach, the transcendentalist-idealist approach and the Marxian approach, philosophy developed new alternatives in order to deal with the new problems that had been raised by these approaches. Partially these approaches were developed further and partially they were opposed by the emergence in reaction to them of new philosophical views. In this way, positivism (Comte, Spencer, Mach), pragmatism (Vaihinger, C. F. S. Schiller, Dewey), neo-Kantianism (Cohen, Cassirer, Windelband, Rickert), the philosophy of life (Schopenhauer, Nietzsche, Bergson, Dilthey), phenomenology and ontology (Husserl, Scheler, Hartmann), and various brands of Marxism (Kautsky, Luxemburg, Plechanov, Lenin) came into existence. Positivism, pragmatism, to a certain extent also neo-Kantianism, especially the Marburg kind, but also in a qualified sense Marxism, more or less, subscribe to science as a means to solve man's problems. It was hoped that the universal application of the scientific method would not only ensure progress, but would also result in a society that would put man in a position to lead the kind of life that would make possible the gratification of all his needs, material, intellectual, cultural and spiritual. The thinkers that subscribed to the other alternatives did not believe in the scientific method as a panacea. They rejected the idea that its universal application would solve the basic problem of the authenticity of human existence. They polemicized that science could not be regarded as fundamental to man's existence, but that a *philosophia prima* would have to start from something deeper, something upon which the sciences themselves depended or something without which there would be no science, e.g., universal values, (Rickert), the will to live (Schopenhauer), the will to power (Nietzsche), the *élan vital* (Bergson), the intentional act (Husserl).

It is now the purpose of this work to investigate the contemporary alternatives that are being offered by philosophy as a means of coping with the world crisis. We hope that it will become clear in the course of our discussions that this crisis is, among others, *a crisis of truth*. Our investigations will be guided by the basic question of the suitability of the offered alternatives for resolving the crisis. The criterion of our judgment shall be whether the respective philosophical alternative has solved the problem of the authenticity of human existence in such a way that man can be said to lead a life in agreement with reality.

We find that the principal alternatives for dealing with the crisis that are being offered by contemporary philosophy are the neo-positivist, the existententialist and the Marxian approach. As now, even within these philosophical alternatives, there are distinct varieties of approach, we shall, in treating them in detail, name them after what appears to us to be their respective fundamental feature. In accordance with this, we shall discuss the neo-positivist approach under the name of *functionalistic alternative*, the existentialist approach under the name of *extential alternative* (why so, we shall state later) and the Marxian alternative under the name of *dialectical alternative*.

We are of the opinion that the neo-Thomist approach is not of decisive importance in this age of secularization and anti-metaphysics, no matter how much we appreciate the attempt of neo-Thomism at providing us with a coherent world-view in these times of mechanization, atomization and piecemeal thinking. This does not mean, however, that we overlook the possibility of a new religious upsurge. But this would be, we think, a spontaneous reaction to the cult of scientism and technologism which is in vogue to-day, rather than the result of the efforts of neo-Thomist thought.

The three principal philosophical alternatives for coping with the present world-crisis as a crisis of truth, now, link up in their turn with their predecessors. The functionalistic alternative links up with the rationalist, the empiricist and the positivist approaches; the existential alternative emerges in reaction to the idealist and transcendentalist approaches; and the dialectical alternative developed from classical Marxism. In spite of this link with their predecessors, which causes the newer theories to retain some of their outstanding features, there is also great deviation from their predecessors, and some of these alternatives were developed in direct opposition to their predecessors. For example, generally speaking, the functionalistic alternative (neo-positivism) was posited in opposition to classical positivism, the exsitential alternative was placed in opposition to idealism, and even in the dialectical alternative to-day (Soviet Marsixm), we find great deviations from classical Marxism.

We shall now proceed with our discussions by trying to establish the nature of the present world-crisis. After having accomplished this task, we shall discuss the previously mentioned philosophical alternatives for dealing with the crisis in close detail and for the following purpose:

1. To show the respective starting point from which each alternative was projected, and the method used in the constitution of its conceptual content.
2. To show in what way each alternative purports to cope with the present crisis and to overcome it.
3. To assess the attempt of each alternative at overcoming the crisis in the light of the question of the authenticity of human existence. For man can hope to cope with the crisis successfully only if he is free in the sense of being in step with reality, for only if he is, are his needs really met, and does he lead an authentic existence. The question is thus: Do the contemporary philosophical alternatives for dealing with the crisis lead man to reality or away from it?
4. To draw conclusions as to the nature of philosophy in general and, in connection with philosophy, to the nature of truth.

THE NATURE OF THE PRESENT CRISIS

From what was said in the *introduction*, it becomes clear that philosophical systems or approaches may be seen as attempts at dealing with the problem of the authenticity of human existence. This means that they are attempts at ordering and arranging the world in such a way that the particular problems and conflicts of a specific historical epoch are "solved" and that so man's needs and interests are met. When man is freed from his wants and conflicts, as he experiences them in a particular historical situation, he is deemed to lead an authentic existence, i.e., an existence in accordance with his true nature. The question now arises what man's true nature really is, and whether his needs can ever be met to the full in reality. There remains the suspicion that man's true nature is established only theoretically, in accordance with a specific approach of a particular philosopher, and that the full gratification of man's needs also occurs in theory only, and thus in the imagination of this particular philosopher.

What is meant thereby is that, in developing his truth-perspective, every philosopher at the same time conceives an image of man, which he regards as man *par excellence.* Thus to give a few examples: The Greeks (notably Plato and Aristotle) regarded man as a *rational being* or *rational animal,* in the sense that he could trace the rational structure of the universe and thus could lead a reasonable life. For Thomas Aquinas, man was a *creature of faith,* who, enlightened by God's wisdom, could recognize God in nature and fuse with God in mystical contemplation. For Descartes, man's essence was *thinking.* Man knew the rational structure of the universe, the moral act and God from clear self-evident ideas in his mind. To Hume, on the other hand, man was a *bundle of sense-impressions,* which, by habitual observation, entered into associations with one another and so caused man to expect the succession and togetherness of the same phenomena again. To Rousseau, man was a being of *natural feeling*, who, by rational intuition, knew his true nature, which was good. In following his natural feeling, man was one with nature and acted morally. Through his natural goodness, he also was blended with the *volonté générale*, i.e., the state as a natural body. Thus many more models of man could be found throughout the history of philosophy.

Our point is now that all these models of man have been conceived in conformity with the philosopher's fundamental premise from which he developed his philosophical project, and that, as such, they are theoretical constitutions, which contradict one another. If authentic existence means an existence in accordance with man's true nature and if man's true nature is derived from the world-view of the respective philosopher, this world-view being different in each particular case, it stands to reason that the problem of authentic existence has not been solved or has been solved in theory and in accordance with the specific world-view or truth-perspective of a particular philosopher only. And if man's authentic existence means an existence in line with reality, it stands to reason that the real ground of the world is also the theoretical conception of a particular philosopher. What is, however, really the real ground of the world if we refer to our examples given above? Is it rational nature, God's wisdom or will, man's thinking or reason? Is it matter or man's experience or man's natural feeling? If no conclusive answer can be given to these questions, then it must be assumed that the theoretical solution of the problem of man's authentic existence is no solution and that the problem remains. If this problem cannot be solved by theoretical constitution, then we must look for another ground of man's authentic existence, one that lies outside all theory, in the field of our actual experience. What we actually experience is the crisis of our own truth as a result of the controversial relation that obtains among our self-constituted truths. From this it follows that man's true nature is controversial and that, therefore, man's authentic existence issues not from theory at all but from practice, namely, the actual controversial relationship that exists between myself and the other. It is precisely this field of the common actual experience of all men by which their truth-perspectives are mutually being called in question and by which are brought to light man's finiteness and limitation, which are the real ground of man's authentic existence. And it is if man complies with this experience and accepts the crisis as the ground of all his creative activity and his continued reorganization of the world in the form of ever new truth-perspectives that he leads an authentic existence. This authentic existence is an ethical existence in the sense that, in recognition of his limitation by the other, the moral act is one of self-restraint and modest self-restriction to the field of his actual experience, which experience he shares with his fellowman and which is their common field of action. In this way, the problem of authentic existence becomes the very ground of man's continued quest for truth. It is not solved by theoretical conceptualization, but is accepted and acknowledged as the real ground of man's creative action. And it is by this very acknowledgment of this problem as insoluble that man is able to lead an authentic existence, i.e., an existence in conformity with his actual experience of the crisis of his own truth as well as his true nature as a controversial being. It is in this sense that man's authentic existence can be defined as an existence in line with reality, a reality which is no longer theoretically constructed, but is actually experienced.

But let these matters rest for a while, we shall still have much to say about this question as our discussion develops. For the time being it is our purpose to call to mind once more that philosophical systems appear to be built with the purpose of solving the problems and overcoming the conflicts of a particular period. These conflicts and contradictions are felt to point to man's estrangement from reality and, as a result of this, to man's self-estrangement. The philosophical alternatives that are offered in this situation purport to lead man back to reality and, by so doing, restore the authenticity of his existence by freeing him from these conflicts. It is of course self-evident that each philosophical system performs this function in a different way, in accordance with the starting-point adopted by a certain philosopher or a certain group of philosophers and in agreement with the specific method that is applied by the respective thinker or thinkers.

In accordance with this, the conception of a philosophical project of whatever kind, at whatever stage of human history, may be seen as an attempt at arranging and ordering our environment in such a way that it becomes meaningful and familiar to man and offers him some kind of orientation and security. In other words, it appears to be the function of philosophy to establish again and again, under changing circumstances of life, the *real ground* of or the *ratio sufficiens* for the world and to deduce from it, under the *principle of identity*, the *authentic character* of man's existence. This "natural" existence of man is at the same time an *ethical existence*, because the highest principle of reality or of truth is every time the greatest good as well. This holds true also in cases where philosophers believe that they have arrived at a scientific truth that is completely neutral and free from all subjective valuing on the part of its knower.[1] But this we shall show when dealing with this particular philosophical approach.

It is thus by making man see truth and reality, as they have been constituted by philosophy, and by so merging him with it, that he is supposed to be free from all conflict, suffering, fear, anxiety, uncertainty and oppression. His needs and wants have been satisfied and his problems are solved. He is at peace with himself and with the world. By comprehending truth and reality, he understands himself, and the authenticity of his existence is restored; for he is now one with the world and with being or, more accurately, what is regarded as the world or as being by the particular philosopher or philosophers. In our *introduction* we observed that the world may be conceived in many ways, as a self-sufficient harmonious cosmos (Plato), as the creation of a perfect being (scholastic philosophy), as the expression of reason (Descartes), as being known by sensation and reflection, i.e., experience (Locke), etc.. Intuition, faith, reason and experience have alternately been seen as the ultimate ground of the world and the key to being and to truth.

As, however, none of the various philosophical approaches that are advanced at a certain historical stage for the purpose of coping with the existing crisis really resolves the crisis because of its inevitably perspectivistic and thus controversial character, by which it enters into a controversial relation with the other philosophical approaches, the crisis seems to be a permanent one. In fact, it is the very permanency of the crisis that causes philosophy to make ever new attempts at overcoming it by the conception of new approaches and by the creation of new concepts in agreement with the particular conditions that happen to prevail at the time.

This brings us to the question of the nature of the contemporary crisis, which has induced philosophy to "solve" man's acute problems and conflicts and to satisfy man's current needs by the great contemporary philosophical projects of neo-positivism, existentialism[2] and Soviet Marxism. Each of these projects must be seen as an alternative of philosophy to cope with the present crisis, which, among others, is a crisis of truth. Naturally, there are differences of opinion and controversy even inside these projects, and some thinkers would resent the

---

[1] It is the logical positivists and the naturalistic linguistic philosophers, for instance, who lay claim to this.

[2] Existentialism is used here in a broad sense. It includes the existentialism proper of Sartre, the philosophy of existence of Jaspers as well as the fundamental ontology of Heidegger.

label we stick upon them. For systematic reasons, however, a certain grouping and labelling cannot be avoided. In so doing, we are guided by the fundamental approach of these philosophical alternatives, such as their *broad* starting-point and the *general* method by which their underlying premises are developed. In neo-positivism it is, roughly speaking, the *functional character of language* which is the starting-point and which is systematically developed or constituted. In existentialism it is the fundamental *phenomenon of human existence as being-there* which is the starting-point and the relationship of which to the world or else to being the respective philosopher seeks to establish by methodological constitution. In Soviet Marxism it is man's *productive activity* which is brought into a *dialectical relation* with the world and in terms of which the process of history is conceived as a *dialectical principle*. It is because of this that we have chosen to deal with these contemporary philosophical alternatives for coping with the crisis of truth under the name of functionalistic, existential and dialectical alternative respectively.

It has been said (by Marcuse, for instance) that the contemporary crisis is due to the power contest between East and the West, which in either camp prevents the full harmonization of the needs and interests of the individuals with those of society. According to Marcuse, monopolistic or selfish interests prevail in either camp. In the West it is those of the big syndicates and in the East it is those of the party functionaries. The use of science and technology for selfish interests of whatever kind causes man to remain unfree. In order to achieve man's freedom from all kind of wants, needs and conflicts and from fear and oppression, a qualitative transformation of society in the West and in the East must take place by a transvaluation of all values, i.e., the freeing of science and technology from monopolistic interests of whatever kind and the translation of spiritual (metaphysical) values, e.g., freedom, into technological values. That is to say, if science and technology were freed from the control and manipulation of certain groups of interest in East and West and were used in the general interest instead of in the private interest of these groups, the present standard and achievements of science and technology would make possible the planning and calculation of the production of material goods in such a way that man's freedom is thereby ensured. By using science and technology in the general interest instead of for the purpose of certain groups to make profit or to stay in power, it would be possible to free man from oppression, war, distress, hunger, anxiety, etc. It is this that Marcuse means by the "quantification of values," and it is by this quantification of values that man's individual interests coincide with the general interest.[3]

An interpretation of the contemporary crisis in terms of the east-west conflict and in terms of individual and collective interest is however in our opinion not the whole truth, but only part of it. It is a mere perspective, which, as is the case with all philosophical perspectives, is controversial, as we shall see when we descuss Marcuse's views in greater detail. Here we only wish to point out that it is highly questionable, whether the scientific and technological methods, while satisfying man's material needs, will gratify to the full man's intellectual, aesthetical and spiritual needs. Marcuse's functionalistic quantification of values and their interpretation as freedom from oppression, war, conflict, fear, anxiety, suffering and want on the negative side and, consequently, liberty, peace, harmony, tranquility, happiness and satisfaction on the positive side are not only very utopian, in as much as thereby man's transformation into a superman is presupposed, but would also entail man's being turned into a machine, robot or computer. As Marcuse himself implies, man's intellectual capacity, his imaginative power (as aesthetical power) would be fully absorbed by scientific and technological planning. His phantasy and imagination would serve as stimuli for the development of more advanced scientific and technological methods to gain even closer control over nature for the benefit of mankind, and his spiritual needs would be abreacted as faith in scientific and technological progress.

In this way, all values would actually be reducible to one common denominator, namely, man's material needs. But surely this transformation of man's intellectual, aesthetical and spiritual needs into material ones and the translation of all values into technological functions give a distorted picture of man and his real needs. They also give a distorted view of the crisis, which is not merely a conflict between East and West and between private and general material interests. It is also a conflict between man and the world, between man and man and between man and himself, as this is shown, for instance, by the philosophy of existence. Generally speaking, the crisis reflects man's struggle and his various efforts of rebuilding the world after the old one had been destroyed in two World Wars. The old values that had been established through classical metaphysics by the marriage between philosophy and religion, reason and faith, history and the state, in short, between truth and reality in the spirit, by which the world was moved,

[3] Cf. Herbert Marcuse, *One-Dimensional Man*

had become obsolete. Taken in a broad way, this kind of thinking dominated the European continent during the 19th century,[4] and largely
corresponded with the social structure of most of the European states.
It also had (through Carlyle, Green, Caird, Bradley and Bosanquet)
great influence in Britain.
After the Second World War, classical metaphysics was definitely out,
and other philosophical approaches were developed in coping with the
task of building a better world and helping man answer the question as
to the nature of his existence in the face of the ruins of his own culture,
which had been bombed to pieces.

The crisis man was facing, was not merely a material crisis, but it
was above all a cultural crisis and as such a *crisis of truth*. For after the
old culture had become extremely doubtful and in fact had collapsed,
a completely fresh start had to be made in the quest for truth. All the
absolute truths that had been conceived by man during the 19th century (and not only the truths of idealist metaphysics) were led *ad absur-
surdum* by the war. This applies not only to Hegel's absolute spirit, by
which history was supposed to be set in motion, but also to the neo-
Kantian norms and values, which were assumed to make man strive for
truth, thus building ever new cultural systems in the direction of truth;
but it also holds true for the positivist myth of progress, i.e., the bringing about of a better world and a better man by the sciences.

Although the natural sciences and technology had revealed their
second face, namely, their destructive side during the war, the war had
also accelerated their growth and development. No wonder then that
the positivist way of thinking survived in philosophy. But in view of
the acute crisis of truth immediately after the Second World War (by
which, because of their destructive nature, the reputation of the sciences and of technology had been greatly undermined) positivist thought
could not continue holding before man's eyes the picture of a promised
land of peace, happiness and prosperity, which the sciences would gradually procure for him. Positivist philosophy could no longer, as it did
in the 19th century, constitute natural laws that were at the same time
laws of history, such as Comte's law of the three stages or Spencer's
law of evolution. This kind of teleological thinking was unacceptable
in the present situation. Thus, in conformity with the call of the time,
positivism re-emerged as neo-positivism. It became purely descriptive and functionalsitic, as we shall yet see. Thereby it hoped to plant

---

[4] Although there was of course much opposition to it by philosophical materialism, positivism and also neo-Kantianism.

man firmly rooted to the earth and by its insistence on "objectivity" and "neutrality" save him the disappointment and frustation which he suffered as a result of his metaphysical and teleological adventures. By this new approach of positivist philosophy, man was to feel more certain again and to regain confidence in himself.

But, as we have already mentioned, by the development of highly destructive weapons, which culminated in the development of deadly nuclear weapons, the sciences had not only proved a blessing but also a menace to human existence. The philosophy of existence felt therefore that nothing was left which could be trusted, no cultural system, no philosophy of history, no scientif'c theory. There was nothing in the world but individual man in his very being-there. He was a stranger in this world, which was hostile to him, in as much as it was essentially different from him, an *en-soi* as opposed to a *pour-soi*, as Sartre would say. Man was nothing himself, ruled by what had become his fundamental feeling, anxiety, which was the very manifestation of his nothingness.

In order to make a fresh start and to determine the authenticity of his existence anew, which would put him in a position to cope with his anxiety, his frustation and his despair, man must not start from *das Seiende* (the objective world) at all, but from himself, from his *Dasein* (being-there). By his *Entschlossenheit*[5] (resolute openmindness to his real situation) or by taking a decision to accept himself as that which he really is, a being-to-death or a being-to-nothing, thus coming to live with this fact and accept it positively as something natural, he could determine himself in the midst of the nothing. It becomes clear that the philosophy of existence rejects both classical metaphysics as well as the sciences. It may be seen as a protest of the individual against any form of self-estrangement and depersonalization, be it by being merged with some historical logos or by being absorbed and levelled by the functionalistic methods of science and technology. As a protest of the individual the philosophy of existence is very much alive[6] In as much as the existential approach to dealing with the current crisis of truth starts from man himself or, alternately, from his consciousness and, especially, in the case of Sartre and Merleau-Ponty,[7]

---

[5] These German terms are those of Heidegger, as he uses them in *Sein und Zeit*.

[6] As a protest it is regarded as such by Fritz Heinemann in his book *Existentialism and the modern Predicament*.

[7] A book to illustrate this is the book of the Dutch philosopher R.C. Kwant, *De Fenomenologie van Merleau-Ponty*, cf. esp. chapter IX "Merleau-Ponty en de Fenomenologie" and chapter XII "Merleau-Ponty en Sartre ".

shows marked traces of transcendentalism and phenomenology, it may be said to link up with idealism in the broad sense of the word. More accurately, it may be said to link up with the *cogito, ergo sum* philosophy of Descartes, Hegel and Husserl, even though it opposes it, and Sartre replaces the *cogito, ergo sum* by the *existo, ergo sum*. In this way, the authentic nature of man's existence is no longer derived from essence, but, conversely, man's essence is derived from his existence.[8]

Soviet Marxism interprets the contemporary crisis of western culture in agreement with its dialectical approach to history. The crisis of western truth, which began to make its appearance already in the 19th century and which was foreshadowed in the writings of Kierkegaard, Schopenhauer and especially Nietzsche, is regarded by Soviet Marxism as resulting from the inevitable contradictions of capitalism. Lenin, the founder of Soviet Marxism, developed Marx's doctrine further and adjusted it to the conditions of his time and to the conditions in Russia. By pointing out that capitalism had reached its extreme stage, namely, that of imperialism, he contended that the labouring class would not be freed and would continue in its self-estrangement (which was imposed upon it by the capitalist way of production) if it entered into any form of compromise with the exploiters, the capitalist class. Consequently, he condemned any kind of "revisionism" or "reformism" by the socialists and the social democrats as a disguise for the continued rule of the capitalists. He polemicized that the working class would be liberated only by revolution, i.e., bringing about the qualitative change of the social structure by force, so bringing it into line with the modern way of production and the true needs of the working class, which represented the majority of the population. Only if the working class, as the productive class, could dispose of its own products, would it become possible for its individual members to lead an authentic existence. To bring about this state of affairs, the communist party must form the vanguard of the working class. It must rouse the political consciousness of its members, and lead it on the way to revolution.[9]

It was as a result of this programme of Lenin's that the Russian socialist party split into a Bolshevik and a Menshevik wing, and in 1912, at the conference in Prague, the Bolsheviki constituted themselves as a party of a new type. Contrary to the expectation of Karl Marx, the

[8] In this regard, cf. G.A. Rauche "Whiter Man?". section 3, in: *The Philosophy of Actuality*.
[9] In regard to this, cf. Lenin's writings "Marxismus und Reformismus", in: *Werke*, vol. 19; "Der Imperialismus als höchstes Stadium des Kapitalismus", in: *Werke*, vol. 22 and "Staat und Revolution", in: *Werke*, vol. 25.

revolution did not take place in those countries that were most advanced in their industrial development, e.g., in England, in France or in Germany, where, according to Marxian dialectic, the negation of the capitalist system by the rapid development of the new productive forces would become apparent and its liquidation a historical necessity. On the contrary, it happend in an industrially underdeveloped country, in Russia. In October 1917, Lenin overthrew the democratic provisional government, which had succeeded the Tsarist regime in spring 1917. When he did so, he predicted that in Germany, too, revolution would break out, and a dictatorship of the proletariat would be established. In accordance with Marx's teaching, he believed that only by the victory of the revolution in a highly advanced capitalist country like Germany, would the Russian revolution be rescued. Marcuse writes on this point "As late as March, 1919, he (Lenin) called the October Revolution a 'bourgeois revolution in so far as the class struggle on the countryside had not yet developed.' And he added that only in the summer of 1918 did the real proletarian revolution on the countryside begin. He clung to the notion that the Russian Revolution must be rescued by the German revolution."[10] The attempt, however, by the German radical leftists, the *Spartakists*, to overthrow the new democratic government that had been formed after the collapse of the German Empire in November 1918 proved abortive. Thus Lenin had to concentrate on Russia alone. From about 1921 onward, the conclusions were drawn from the failure of the German revolution, and, in view of the increasing power of the U. S. A. , Lenin now saw the possibility that the Soviet state, for a long time, might have to coexist with capitalism. In conformity with Russia being largely an agricultural country, he modified Marxism by proclaiming the alliance between the industrial workers and the peasants. Marcuse says: "But it is precisely Lenin's belief in the tentative and preliminary character of the Russian Revolution which leads him to formulations clearly foreshadowing the Stalinist policy. Socialism presupposes capitalism - or at least the achievements of capitalism, namely, a high degree of industrialization, a high productivity of labor, and a highly developed, skilled, and disciplined labor force."[11]

It was these aims of a totalitarian doctrine that justified the retention of a totalitarian state and the control of the state by the communist party, which would be in effect the control of the state by the par-

[10] *Soviet Marxism*, p. 43.
[11] Op. cit., p. 43.

ty's secretary. It is not surprising then that, under Lenin's successor, Stalin, Soviet Marxism, assumed more and more the character of a one man dictatorship. By ruthlessly liquidating all opponents and possible rivals, Stalin concentrated on the development of heavy industries at the expense of the production of consumer's goods. During the Second World War, Russian Communism became more nationalistic and patriotic in outlook, and immediately after the war the thesis was propounded of socialism in one land.

The reaction to Stalinist rule came after Stalin's death in 1935 in the form of the brief period of the thaw. But when Khrushchev took over, one man rule was restored under the guise of de-Stalinization and the breaking down of the Stalinist cult of *the* person. In foreign policy, too, Khrushchev skilfully disguised his true aim of communist expansion by proclaiming the thesis of coexistence between communism and capitalism. The present division of power in the Soviet Union between the head of the government and the secretary of the communist party has not resulted in a new thaw. On the contrary, there is every sign of a freeze up, especially in the face of growing discontent with Soviet rule and Soviet philosophy particularly among the Soviet intelligentsia, where there are marked individualistic tendencies, and among the satellite states with their national aspirations. All in all, we may at this stage say this much in regard to Soviet Marxism: The inherent crisis in the Soviet camp in itself casts doubt on the central thesis of Soviet Marxism, namely, that the establishment of the dictatorship of the proletariat by the communist party is a necessary interim measure on the road to communism. Is it humanly possible to reach this aim at all? Or is it in conflict with human nature and not really representative of man's true needs? We shall try to answer these questions in our discussion of the dialectical alternative of philosophy for coping with the crisis of truth.

If we have presented the three philosophical approaches of neo-positivism, existentialism and Soviet Marxism as alternatives for dealing with the crisis of truth, which became extremely acute after the First World War and has since grown in intensity, the question now arises as to the effectuality of each in dealing with this crisis. Has it been overcome by any of these alternatives? Has man, in the light of the one or the other, re-discovered the authenticity of his existence? Does any of them satisfy his true needs? If our answer to these questions is no, it must at this stage be considered as preliminary, for it is encumbent on us to show in greater detail why these philosophical approaches have failed to deal effectively with this crisis. The reason why we give this answer at this stage already is because these three philosophical approaches are controversial and contradictory, and therefore call each other in question. By their controversial and contradictory character, they constitute a crisis themselves. As they may be said to represent a different concern of man and have been developed from a particular premise, they are mere perspectives or aspects of truth and cannot therefore lay claim to having overcome the crisis of truth, nor can they be regarded as having given a satisfactory answer to the question of the authenticity of human existence. They cannot be said to have solved the problem of human freedom either. On the contrary, by laying claim to the total character of their doctrine, their mutual contradiction is as total. They are determined not to tolerate one another or to be open to each other, but they are bent on destroying each other. In other words, the total character of their mutual contradiction could cause the contemporary crisis to develop into a catastrophe with far more disastrous consequences than those of the last war. The total contradiction that, because of their total character, exists among the contemporary philosophical alternatives for coping with the crisis of truth causes the *natural* crisis that exists among all men, nations and human truth-perspectives to assume a malignant character.

That the three philosophical approaches to resolving the crisis have failed to deal with the present crisis of truth is also shown by the fact that other alternatives for dealing with this crisis have been developed in the face of them, in outspoken criticism and contradiction. This is further proof that by them man's needs and wants have not been satisfied, and the problem of the authenticity of his existence has not been solved. In this connection the questions arise: Will man's needs ever be satisfied, will his conflicts ever be solved and will the question of the authenticity of his existence ever be answered by the constitution of philosophical truth of whatever kind? These questions can be answered only after a closer investigation has been made of the three leading philosophical alternatives, which are at present grappling with these problems, namely, the functionalistic, existential and dialectical alternative. This is perhaps best accomplished by referring chiefly to typical representatives of these alternatives, making mention of other representatives as the necessity for doing so arises.

THE FUNCTIONALISTIC ALTERNATIVE OR THE ALTERNATIVE OF THE *STATUS QUO*

The functionalistic alternative for dealing with the present crisis of truth is best illustrated by the thought of Ludwig Wittgenstein. The development of his thought compromises the stage of logical positivism, as it appears in his *Tractatus Logico-Philosophicus*, and the stage of linguistic philosophy, as it is propounded in his *Philosophical Investigations*. Although there are marked differences in these two works, implying a definite change in Wittgenstein's thought, both Wittgenstein's logical positivist and linguistic approach have that in common that they are functionalistic by nature. Wittgenstein's approach has proved very appealing to western philosophy and to Anglo-Saxon thought in particular. Wittgenstein was a pupil of Russell and a member of the Vienna circle, whose members grouped themselves around Moritz Schlick. The Vienna circle developed further the functionalistic or symbolic approach of Whitehead's and Russel's *Principia Mathematica*. This functionalistic approach is still very powerful on the European continent, but has even greater influence in the Anglo-Saxon world. Carnap, Reichenbach, Ayer, Ryle and Austin are the most outstanding representatives of this philosophical approach.

Why now do we call the method of logical positivism and that of linguistic philosophy functionalistic? The answer is because they have that in common with the natural sciences that they *describe* processes or events, or else examine *functions*, i.e., the function of language. They purport not to theorize *about* anything, the world, life, man, language, or to ask questions *about* the phenomena of the world, which cannot be answered and therefore are nonsensical. "Most propositions and questions," says Wittgenstein, "that have been written about philosophical matters, are not false, but senseless. We cannot, therefore, answer questions of this kind at all, but only state their senselessness. Most questions and propositions of the philosophers result from the fact that we do not understand the logic of our language .... And so it is not to be wondered at that the deepest problems are really *no* problems."[1]

The logic of our language is, however, determined by what Wittgenstein calls *facts*, i.e., not things, but natural events or processes. That is to say, our language is meaningful only as long as it records these facts. Wittgenstein writes: "The gramophone record, the musical thought, the score, the waves of sound, all stand to one another in that pictorial internal relation, which holds between language and the world."[2] It is thus impossible to say anything *about* the world if we are embedded in the world. If we do attempt to do that, we ask meaningless questions and create mock-problems. If our speech is supposed to have meaning, it must restrict itself to the recording of *facts*, which can be combined into *atomic facts*. It is the function of language to record what is the case, and, according to Wittgenstein, the limits of our meaningful language are clearly circumscribed, as transpires from the following: "The world is everything that is the case. The world is the totality of facts, not of things. The world is determined by the facts, and by these being *all* the facts. For the totality of facts determines both what is the case, and also all that is not the case. The facts in logical space are the world. The world divides into facts. Any one can either be the case or not be the case, and everything else remain the same"[3]

From this it follows that our statements of empirical facts are logical only in as much as they are truth-functions of the world, as that which is the case. As we are imbedded in the world through our language, we must not elevate ourselves above the world as a subject. If this is done all the same, we arrive at mock-questions and create mock-problems. We then betake ourselves into the sphere of the ineffable, i.e., into the province of ethics or of metaphysics. As we are embedded in the experiental world, we must not reflect on it. If we do reflect on it, we transgress or transcend our empirical limit; and if we put our reflections into words, we talk nonsense. That is why Wittgenstein, too, talks nonsense as long as he reflects on the world. "My propositions," he writes, "are elucidatory in this way: he who understands me finally recognizes them as senseless, when he has climbed out through them, on them, over them. (He must so to speak throw away the ladder, after he has climbed up on it.) He must surmount these propositions;

---

[1] *Tractatus Logico-Philosophicus*, 4.003.
[2] *Op. cit., 4.014.*
[3] *Op. cit., 1-1.21.*

then he sees the world rightly. Whereof one cannot speak, thereof one must be silent."[4]

Man's being embedded in the world, therefore, forbids him to constitute the world as an absolute. Wittgenstein has recognized that such constitution of the world as a result of the question about the world, i.e., its structure, essence or its *real ground*, is nothing but the subject (man) constituting itself. This act is what the Germans call *Faktizität*, by which is meant the constitution of the world or the absolute in man's consciousness as an immanent truth. The method of constituting the world in our mind in some way or other was used by philosophy prior to the advent of functionalistic thinking. It was applied in a transcendental way by Kant and from the idealist standpoint in the metaphysics of the 19th century (Fichte, Hegel, Schelling).[5] It is the latter that is attacked most vehemently by functionalistic philosophy. But phenomenology and ontology, too, make use of this method. Husserl, Scheler and Hartmann constitute the world by regarding consciousness as the ground from which the world is *meaningfully* constituted and its structure is determined. In spite of differences as to how the mind (subject) is related to the world (object), i.e., whether it is the mind that acts on the world (Husserl's intentional acts) or whether it is the world (being) that affects the mind (Scheler's and Hartmann's idea of the *resistance* of the world or of man's mind being *affected* by the world) the essence or structure of the world, in each case, is arrived at by *eidetic reduction* or *ideation*, i.e., by deriving the meaning and and structure of the world from man's conscious action or reaction. Distinguishing clearly between the existing world, *das Seiende* and being, *das Sein*, Heidegger, like Wittgenstein, criticizes this method of attempting to arrive at the absolute by the constitution of the world, *das Seiende*, in our consciousness, but for reasons that are entirely different from those of Wittgenstein, as we shall soon see. His starting-point being the opposite of that of Wittgenstein, it is not surprising that he draws conclusions which fall outside Wittgenstein's empirical limit (as we have shown it above) and for this reason would be regarded as meaningless by Wittgenstein. According to Wittgenstein, philosophy must by reflection abolish itself. It has no explanatory or teaching function, but only an analytical one. Wittgenstein says: "The object

---

[4] *Tractatus Logico-Philosophicus*, 6.54–7.

[5] It is interesting to note that Schelling, esp. in his later works, recognizes that, because of the finite nature of the constitutive act, the world that is thereby constituted cannot be absolute and self-sufficient. He thus asks the question of the ultimate ground of the world, which remains outside all constitution.

of philosophy is the logical clarification of thoughts. Philosophy is not theory but activity. A philosophical work consists essentially of elucidations. The result of philosophy is not a number of 'philosophical propositions', but to make propositions clear."[6]

In order to avoid the constitution of the world in our consciousness, which amounts to the constitution of the human self in an absolute dimension, Wittgenstein brackets the self or consciousness. He regards language as something objective, in the sense of recording or describing our experience of the world (natural events) in a meaningful way. When I speak meaningfully, I speak of natural processes. It is in this sense that propositions are truth-functions of our experience as an experience of that which is the case, and it is by arriving at these truth-functions through the clarification of scientific propositions that Wittgenstein's method reveals itself as atomistic and functionalistic. Wittgenstein's linguistic atomism corresponds to Russell's sense-data atomism. And just as Russell is chiefly interested in the sense-data of the sciences, which he seeks to connect logically with one another, Wittgenstein is primarily interested in scientific propositions and their functional relations to one another.

It may be argued that Wittgenstein's negative approach in regard to philosophy and the strict limitation of question and answer and therefore of meaningful propositions to the sphere of the intelligible, i.e., of science, were meant to mark off more clearly the realm of the ineffable. Indeed, there are thinkers, Walter Schulz, for example, who say that in Wittgenstein's thought this sharp separation of the ineffable from the world is essential for the determination of the mystical. Schulz formulates it as follows: "Welt ist Dimension von Tatsachen, bezugsweise von Elementen der Tatsachen, den Sachverhalten, und das Mystische ist das Nicht-Tatsächliche, das heisst der 'absolute,' für sich bestehende Sinn, der als solcher eben nicht fassbar ist."[7] From Wittgenstein's propositions: "We feel that even if *all possible* scientific questions be answered, the problems of life have still not been touched at all. Of course there is then no question left, and just this is the answer. The solution of the problem of life is seen in the vanishing of this problem..... There is indeed the inexpressible. This *shows* itself, it is mystical,"[8] Schulz draws the conclusion that Wittgenstein wanted to characterize the mystical as that which exists as the immediate, because here all questioning ceases or, more ac-

---

[6] *Tractatus Logico-Philosophicus*, 4.112.
[7] *Wittgenstein, Die Negation der Philosophie*, p.45.
[8] *Tractatus-Logico-Philosophicus*, 6.52–6.522.

curately, has never really started.[9] This does not mean that Schulz regards Wittgenstein as a transcendental philosopher, as is done by Stegmüller or Habermas, for example. This view is categorically rejected by Schulz. It merely means that Schulz polemicizes that Wittgenstein's distinction between the sphere of life and the sphere of science in the *Tractatus* is out of step with the times, and that the interpretation of Wittgenstein as a transcendental philosopher goes against Wittgenstein's declared aim, namely, to eliminate subjectivity and to negate philosophy altogether. Also against this aim goes the attempt of the Oxford and Cambridge linguistic schools to provide philosophy with a new foundation by means of "language games" from a fixed position. Schulz seeks to show the dubiousness of the idea of language games, as put forward by Wittgenstein in the *Philosophical Investigations*. He points out that Wittgenstein uses an extreme definition of language, which we would call the functional aspect of language, as the criterion by which he judges the meaningfulness of all communication. Schulz draws our attention to the primitive nature of Wittgenstein's arguments and to his utter failure to understand phenomena such as mind, reason, etc. According to Schulz the *Philosophical Investigations* do not really constitute a new advance, but keep moving at the level of vague ambiguity.

In spite of the plausible possibility of seeing him not primarily as a positivist, but rather as a mystic, as one who really means to show us how little we know and how little we can say intelligibly in contradistinction to that which cannot be spoken about, e.g., the world as a whole, happiness, life and death, and which, therefore, is beyond philosophical questioning, Wittgenstein the logical positivist and Wittgenstein the linguist have had a greater influence upon contemporary western thought than Wittgenstein the mystic has had. This is no mere coincidence. The situation between the World Wars, and particularly the situation after the Second World War, was such that man's greatest concern was the need for security and for certainty. This need had risen to a climax after the final collapse of the old cultural values and the break-down of classical metaphysics. In addition, any kind of telelogical thinking both in history and in the sciences had lost credit in the light of new scientific discoveries, e.g., the growing scientific insight into the structure of the atom, which simultaneously increased our wonder and our puzzlement. It upset established scientific theories and concepts. Max Planck's quantum theory and Werner Heisenberg's

---

[9] *Wittgenstein, Die Negation der Philosophie*, p.46.

relation of uncertainty, for instance, called in question the classical concept of causality, which had seen the basic structure of the world in the reciprocal cause and effect relation. This relation had lent to the world unity, homogeneity and continuity, which now lay shattered to pieces by the new discoveries in nuclear physics. Albert Einstein's theory of relativity, too, shook the old scientific picture of the world to its roots. Space and time, for instance, were no longer perceptual forms or concrete realities, but, in their combination as space-time, assumed the functionalistic role of a fourth dimension and became metrical in character. This fourth dimension consisted in the functional relations by which events were referred to one another and which were laid down in terms of mathematical formulae.[10] Small wonder, then, that, in the face of such an atomized world, the question about truth was asked afresh; for only if this question were to be answered in some way or other, would man be able to answer the question as to the authenticity of his existence as well. In other words, man's question about truth always occurs in a situation of crisis, i.e., from the experience of conflict and the feeling of uncertainty. And his question about truth becomes particularly insistent when the crisis sharpens and the conflict increases, as it happened in between the two World Wars and is still happening to-day. It becomes understandable that philosophy, as the discipline that is supposed to give an answer to man's question about truth in general, gave this answer in the negative, i.e., by negating itself.

It is now by its very self-negation that philosophy turns into the functionalistic alternative or the alternative of the *status quo* in its attempt at coping with the current crisis of truth. By exercising a mere analytical function in regard to propositions describing natural events, or else by becoming descriptive of the various kinds of human experience, philosophy practically identifies itself with the scientific method or rather conforms to it. In this way, the scientific method becomes universal or the method *par excellence*, for it eventually comes to be applied by philosophy to all kinds of human experience, scientific, aesthetical, ethical and religious experience. Philosophy, therefore, is no longer creative and constitutive, as was the philosophy of

---

[10] There are attempts in philosophy, e.g., the attempt of Samuel Alexander in his work *Space, Time and Deity*, to conceive space-time as the "stuff of the world" and to constitute the universe from this principle of pure motion. According to this philosophy, the world "emerges" from this principle of pure motion in this order: Physico-chemical processes, the process of life, consciousness, which by the experience of "duration" points towards the future and thus to "emergents" of a higher order.

the past. By tracing the logical functions of propositions, which record our experience, philosophy, just like contemporary science, becomes atomistic and functionalistic.

Philosophy, in its form of logical positivism, also has that in common with the sciences that it insists that meaningful propositions must be verifiable in terms of objective empirical evidence. Wittgenstein, we have already observed, holds that meaningful propositions should be verified by facts (natural events). R. Carnap believes that the function of verification is performed by intersubjective protocols, i.e., statements the content of which rests exclusively upon direct observations about physical events.[11] A. J. Ayer believes that verification is effected by synthetical sense-data propositions, i.e., sense-data propositions, so to speak, serve as evidence for propositions about material things.[12] G. J. Warnock, in a similar way, argues that the relation that holds between sense-data propositions and propositions about material things is that of verdict and evidence.[13] Both Ayer and Warnock are severely criticized by J. L. Austin in *Sense and Sensibilia*, a book which Warnock compiled from Austin's lecture notes. Reichenbach, on the other hand, turned against his former associates of the Vienna Circle on the question of verifiability. He denies that empirical verifiability can lend certainty to our propositions. His statistical If-Then-Always propositions as veridical propositions, such as, heat always flows from a warmer to a colder body, have only the value of *probability*. According to Reichenbach, a proposition is meaningful only if the degree of its probability can be determined, i.e., if its probability can be verified.[14]

By examining the truth-functions of propositions, and those of scientific propositions in particular, philosophy strives hard to avoid any kind of subjectivity and to rule out any subjective valuation, as they are bound to occur as long as philosophy is creative and constitutive. By conforming to the method of the natural sciences, philosophy seeks to avoid meaningless questions and mock-problems. It endeavours to arrive at an objectivity by which certainty is restored, even if, as in the case of Reichenbach, this certainty is a matter of degree. The question of truth is answered not by the constitutive activity of philosophy,

---

[11] Carnap, "Die physikalische Sprache als Universalsprache der Wissenschaft", in: *Erkenntnis*, 2, 1932.
[12] Cf. *The Foundations of Empirical Knowledge*.
[13] Cf. his book entitled *Berkeley*, chapters 7–9.
[14] Cf. *Wahrscheinlichkeitslehre*, but, also, *The Rise of Scientific Philosophy*.

but by not asking the question at all.[15] In other words, philosophy no longer philosophizes (in the sense of contemplates) about truth, but merely analyses or describes the truth-functions of propositions. Henceforth the question no longer is: What is truth?, but: How do propositions work? That is to say, when are propositions meaningful and how are they functionally (logically) related to one another? This corresponds to the scientific question of how atoms function, which is answered by measuring atomic events and describing their functional relations in terms of mathematical formulae. By this method, too, we shall obtain no answer as to what an atom is, i.e., whether it is spiritual or material by nature. Thus any kind of "what-question," be it about truth or about atoms, which aims at essence or quality, is dismissed as non-sensical and is replaced by the "how-question," which aims at function and quantity.

It is by conforming to the natural sciences that philosophy, in its attempt at coping with the crisis of truth, reveals itself as the *functionalistic alternative* or the *alternative of the status quo*. For by conforming to the natural sciences, it conforms not only to the material needs of modern scientific and technological man, but it also renounces any attempt at constituting the world as a coherent whole, lest it should provide us with a new *Weltanschauung* that will give rise to new controversy and cause fresh conflict, doubt and uncertainty. By contenting itself with the mere analysis of propositions, philosophy keeps the *status quo* and by so doing hopes to overcome the crisis of truth by blending man into the world of functional processes. Standing in an immediate functional or operational relation with the world, man becomes a functionalistic being *par excellence*. The functional relation, so to speak, becomes the substance of the world. It is determined in terms of mathematics, in which form it allows man to exercise functional control over the world and to change it at will by improving his functional skill all the time. His increasing functional control over the world gives him the feeling of power, certainty and self-confidence. It makes him develop great faith in progress and rouses in him the idea that on principle nothing is impossible for him, that it is only a question of time before his knowledge of nature will be complete. In this way, a cult of the sciences and of technology is developed by man, which causes his thinking to be governed and dominated by the sciences and by technology. It is a subtle way of brainwashing him, by

---

[15] The fact, however, that the problem of truth is settled by not asking the question about truth implies this question.

which the forces that are supposed to assist him to lead a better life and to become a better man begin to overpower him and turn him into their slave. Already Friedrich Nietzsche had foreseen that such a process might occur. He called it the *comedia humana*. The poet-philosopher Franz Kafka described it in his novels, which may be regarded as a documentation of the disease of our time. But, alas, little does man realize the fallacy of his almost religious belief in the sciences and technology and the dangers such blind faith harbours. Intoxicated by his scientific and technological success, man loses all sound sense of proportion, throws caution to the winds and dismisses as unfounded pessimism all realistic reference to his natural limits. We shall come back to this topic at a later stage.

For the time-being, it is our object to show how, by blending man with the functional or operational world, philosophy seeks to solve man's burning problems, i.e., the problem of truth, of authentic existence, of the whole of life and death and of happiness. It may be said that the functionalistic alternative for coping with the present crisis of truth "solves" these problems by not accepting them as problems or by not letting them become problems. That is to say, it solves them by not asking any questions about them or, which amounts to the same thing, by not contemplating them. These problems, so to speak, will solve themselves, as our functional skill improves and as, thereby, the world is increasingly brought under our functional control. Thus the question of the authenticity of human existence, too, resolves itself in as much as it reveals itself as a functionalistic existence; for, by the improvement of his functional skill, man's basic needs, material, intellectual and spiritual, will be satisfied to an ever larger extent. This must be so because, as man increases his functional control over the world, he increases his material comfort and his functional knowledge, which in turn strengthens his faith in progress. The pleasure and happiness that man experiences as a result of the improvement of his functional skill and his growing control over the world also solve the problem of value.

It becomes obvious that the functionalistic alternative for coping with the crisis of truth is an alternative of the *status quo*, in as much as it makes man see himself as an integrated member of the functionalistic or technological society. It is an alternative of the *status quo* in as much as it purports to satisfy all of man's needs through the very technological structure of this society. Any philosophical alternative, therefore, that suggests the qualitative or structural change of this society may be regarded as giving the signal for a revolution which would disturb peaceful evolution and the further extension of man's functional skill, by which, eventually, all problems, conflicts and contradictions would be solved.[16]

We have already mentioned that Wittgenstein's thinking did not remain the same. In the *Tractatus Logico-Philosophicus* his approach was that of logical positivism. In the *Philosophical Investigations*, he changed over to linguistic philosophy. It is not our purpose here to examine in how far the *Philosophical Investigations* link up with the *Tractatus* and in how far they deviate from it. Our purpose is to show that, despite marked differences, the latter is as functionalistic as is the former and, for this reason, forms a branch of the functionalistic alternative for dealing with the crisis of truth. It is thus self-evident that linguistic philosophy has that in common with logical positivism that it, too, lends itself to the retention of the *status quo*.

Walter Schulz sees the divergent tendency of the *Philosophical Investigations* from the *Tractatus* as follows: In the *Tractatus*, Wittgenstein still sought to elucidate his procedure methodically by philosophical propositions (which, in the end, he declared to be senseless). Such reflection is now to be ruled out completely; for every kind of self-reflection is now to be excluded in favour of thinking without presuppositions of any kind. This particular type of thought can only consist in describing the behaviour (function) of language and nothing else. If Wittgenstein in the *Tractatus* still asserted that he had solved certain problems, such a statement could no longer be made in the *Philosopical Investigations*, simply because there are no more problems left in the "language games," according to the rules of which the meaning of words and propositions is now determined. In other words, there is no longer a model language as there was still in the *Tractatus* in the form of scientific language. It is now ordinary language the meaning of which is investigated in accordance with how it is used under specific conditions and in a particular context. Apart from the versatile functions that words fulfil and the many various ways in which an expression such as "game" or "real," for instance, can be used, there is a certain

---

[16] Herbert Marcuse in his book *One-Dimensional Man*, pp.108–114, gives examples of how the functionalistic establishment, in the interest of those who control the technological means of production, seeks to keep the *status quo* by "operational thinking", i.e., by the reduction of "vague" general statements such as the "wages are too low" to the specific individual circumstances of those by whom this complaint was raised. By "taking care" of these individual cases and by improving their circumstances, the conflict is "solved". By "solving" it in this individual manner, the conflict is deprived of its general significance as a symptom of fundamental contradictions within the functionalistic society as a whole, which contradictions point to the need for a qualitative or structural change of society.

way of talking in conformity with man's versatile activities. A logician, for instance, plays a definite language game according to certain set of rules. A scientist would use signs, words and propositions in a specific manner. The form of language he uses would not be used by the poet, for example, and vice versa; in fact, if this were done, language would become meaningless. If this idea of language games is taken to its logical conclusion, a distinction can be made between ordinary talk, scientific talk, logical talk, moral talk, poetical or artistic talk, theological talk, etc. It becomes so clear that the meaning of words and propositions is now determined in accordance with their specific function of recording our particular activities or experience. In this way, language comes to be regarded as describing or giving expression to man's forms of life in a *neutral* manner, i.e., as giving expression to man's versatile experience of the world.

Philosophy, by theorizing about the world and about language, used words in a way which was different from their common usage. By trying to explain and by forming concepts about the world and about human experience, instead of merely describing this experience, philosophy bewitched the world and so misled man. It was in this way that meaningless questions were asked and mock-problems created. Wittgenstein says: "We may not advance any kind of theory. There must be not anything hypothetical in our considerations. We must do away with all *explanation*, and description alone must take its place..... The problems are solved, not by giving new information, but by arranging what we have always known. Philosophy is a battle against the bewitchment of our intelligence by means of language."[17] If philosophy uses words such as "knowledge," "being," "object," "self," etc. and seeks to comprehend the essence of a thing, one must always ask the question whether, in the natural ordinary language, this particular word is ever really used in this way. "What *we* do is to bring words back from their metaphysical to their everyday use."[18]

According to Wittgenstein, therefore, philosophy has not a theoretical, but only an elucidatory or analytical function to fulfil in regard to that which is already given by our language. It does not change anything, but leaves everything as it is. Instead of theorizing about language, it merely determines its truth-function in accordance with man's authentic experience, e.g., the experience of a lover, a baker, a scientist, etc. By assigning to philosophy a mere analytical function in

---

[17] *Philosophical Investigations*, paragraph 109.
[18] *Op. cit.*, paragraph 116.

regard to the use of language in concrete situations, all philosophical problems disappear. Wittgenstein says: "A philosophical problem has the form: 'I don't know my way about.' Philosophy may in no way interfere with the actual use of language; it can in the end only describe it.For it cannot give it any foundation either. It leaves everything as it is. It also leaves mathematics as it is, and no mathematical discovery can advance it. A 'leading problem of mathematical logic' is for us a problem of mathematics like any other."[19]

We thus become aware that Wittgenstein, in the *Philosophical Investigations*, pleads for the self-negation of philosophy even more consistently than he did in the *Tractatus*, this time in favour of ordinary language. Schulz remarks that it would be appropriate to say that the general tendency of the self-destruction of philosophy finds expression in the concrete problems of language games. The functionalistic nature of the language game becomes evident by the know-how-to-play-the-game. That is to say, in playing the game, a knowledge of the rules of the game is required. If this requirement is met and if the rules are observed, then philosophical problems melt like butter in the sun. Wittgenstein puts it as follows: "The real discovery is the one that makes me capable of stopping doing philosophy when I want to. - The one that gives philosophy peace, so that it is no longer tormented by the questions which bring *itself* in question. - Instead, we now demonstrate a method, by examples; and the series of examples can be broken off. - Problems are solved (difficulties eliminated), not a *single* problem. There is not *a* philosophical method, though there are indeed methods, like different therapies."[20]

As in the *Tractatus* I was conceived as being embedded in the world by scientific propositions, which it was philosophy's business to analyze, so I am now embedded in the world by everyday language. The therapeutic method, which consists in the abandonment of philosophical questions, will replace philosophy by the various language games i.e., the versatile manner of using signs, words and propositions in various concrete situations of life. As we have already pointed out, the description of how a word is used under certain conditions reveals definite forms of life. From this Wittgenstein draws the conclusion that "every sentence in our language 'is in order as it is' " and "where there

---

[19] *Philosophical Investigations*, paragraphs 123–124.
[20] *Op.cit.*,paragraph 133   (In this regard, also cf. J. L. Austin's *Sense and Sensibilia*, in which Austin, by showing the versatile meaning of words in the concrete situation, seeks to lead *ad absurdum* Ayer's dichotomies, e.g., the dichotomy of material thing and sense-datum.)

is sense there must be perfect order. -So there must be perfect order even in the vaguest sentence."[21]

We realize that the meaning of the world (truth) and of life (action) is revealed in everyday language by the functional nature of words. The authenticity of our existence cannot be determined by philosophical theories or systems, but reveals itself in the functional nature of our language, in the sense that the description of the versatile functions of words at the same time reveals man's way of life in terms of his manifold activities. Any kind of human activity or experience, be it of a private, professional, scientific, artistic or religious nature, can be included under a specific language game. In this way, contradictions are rendered harmless, nay, become one of the conditions or presuppositions for playing the game meaningfully. In this manner, linguistic philosophy too, by its functionalistic nature, becomes a philosophy of the *status quo*, i.e., a philosophical alternative that attempts to overcome the present crisis by supporting the functionalistic way of thinking of contemporary technological society. By the great variety of language games that are played, linguistic philosophy, too, seeks to give satisfaction to man's basic needs, material, intellectual, aesthetical and spiritual. By making contradiction the very condition for playing the language game in a meaningful way, functionalistic society need not fear contradiction as a danger, as calling in question its fundamental structure. By being included in the functionalistic system itself, contradiction becomes even one of the main props of the functionalistic system and hence of the *status quo*.

After discussing the linguistic starting-point and the therapeutic method of the functionalistic alternative for dealing with the crisis of truth and after showing how this alternative proposes to overcome the crisis, we now ask the question, whether, by this method, the crisis has been settled? For this purpose it becomes necessary to assess this method, particularly in the light of the question of authentic existence. There are critics of the functionalistic alternative and its therapeutic method, for instance Ernest Gellner and Herbert Marcuse, who must be mentioned here, because their criticism throws light upon some of the shortcomings of the functionalistic alternative.

Gellner sees the difference between logical positivism and linguistic philosophy as follows: Logical positivism works according to a model, namely, the dichotomy of "reports of experiential fact, whose claim to truth resides exclusively in that the facts bear them out; and, secondly,

[21] *Philosophical Investigations*, paragraph 98.

logic, interpreted as the consequences of calculations within systems whose rules are conventionally established."[22] Linguistic philosophy, now, overcomes logical positivism not by argument, but by refusing to accept its underlying model. It does so by shifting from the standpoint of the First Person view of knowledge (epistemological approach) to the Third Person picture of language. It is true that this Third Person picture of language was already present in logical positivism, but there it was associated with the First Person approach. Linguistic philosophy now "destroys or prejudges the First Person vision of knowledge, and in the second step destroys or prejudges the simplicity of the already more-or-less Third Person picture of language (in logical positivism) by insisting on taking note of the complexity of actual language. The first step.... is based mainly on refusing to look at things in any way other than the Third Person one, by insisting on the natural standpoint that takes the world for granted, and by claiming.... that deviations from it are the pathology of language."[23] Thus linguistic philosophy "overcomes" logical positivism "by refusing to allow the knower, or the language he uses, to be pivotal, central, to be creators of the world: on the contrary, it sees both him and the language he uses inescapably as processes or events *in* the world. In so doing, it takes the world for granted."[24]

On the whole, Gellner's criticism of linguist philosophy in his book *Words and Things* could be summed up as follows: Gellner shows that linguistic philosophy is a cult of ordinary language, leading to mystical revelations. He refutes its claim to absolute objectivity, in that it pretends not to follow a preconceived model or to be a theory about anything, the world, knowledge, language, by pointing out the *principles* that underly its naturalistic approach to language and by showing that its views on language, the world and philosophy are *valid* only in terms of these principles. Among these he finds the argument of the Paradigm Case, the generalized version of the Naturalistic Fallacy, the Contrast Theory of Meaning and the doctrine of Polymorphism. By chiefly referring to the writings of Ludwig Wittgenstein, Gellner succeeds in showing that the naturalistic approach to language implies a theory *about* language and a standard of value to which linguistic philosophy

[22] *Words and Things*, p.87.
[23] *Op.cit.*, p. 93.
[24] *Op.cit.*, p.92   (Examples of this kind of thinking are G. Ryle's *The Concept of Mind* and *Dilemmas* as well as J.L. Austin's *Sense and Sensibilia* and *Philosophical Papers*. It takes its origin in the philosophy of G.E. Moore, especially in Moore's essay, "The Refutation of Idealism," in: *Mind*, 1903).

subscribes, two things that are categorically denied by linguistic philosophers. The implication by it of a standard of value causes linguistic philosophy to succumb to the Naturalistic Fallacy itself; for this implication means the presence of a subjective element, which detracts from its strictly "scientific" and "neutral" character. It becomes thus clear that linguistic philosophy moves in a circle. By dogmatically insisting on the ordinary language approach and by asserting that by the observation of the rules of language or the function of words man's experience of the world is accurately described, linguistic philosophy does imply a specific theory of language; for that the function of language and its relation with the world can be seen in a different way is already proof that the specific approach of lingusitic philosophy is one theory about language and its relation with the world as against many others. Gellner may therefore be said to have shown that linguistic philosophy is a theory among theories, a method among other methods of constituting truth. As such it does influence man's attitude towards life and his way of acting. Gellner, however, goes much further in his criticism of linguistic philosophy. He reveals the arbitrary and fallacious character of the previously mentioned principles, and, by taking the principal arguments of linguistic philosophers to their logical conclusion, exposes their triviality, their ambiguity and their contradictoriness. By emphasizing that the plausibility and thus the great appeal of linguistic philosophy lies in its very arbitrariness and dogmatism and by showing that it is this very plausibility that is misleading, Gellner exorcizes the spell which this kind of philosophy is still casting on many a thinker to-day. If naturalistic linguistic philosophy affects to be a cure of the philosophical disease of asking unanswerable questions, Gellner's revelation of linguistic philosophy as a myth of common sense and a cult of ordinary language frees us from the spell which it might hold over us and from the temptation that lies in its *Argument from Impotence*, i.e., the self-negation of philosophy. Gellner lays his finger on the basic error of linguistic philosophy, which consists in the assumption that thought is bound by the kind of language game it employs. According to him, the opposite is true. Genuine thought consists in what linguistic philosophy regards as the "pathology" of language, namely, in continually reassessing our terms and our norms that are built into it as the presupposition for intellectual advancement. By pointing out that new discoveries seldom, if ever, move within a pre-established language game, Gellner has torn asunder the chains by which linguistic philosophy has been fettering man's thought for decades, thus making him conform to the *status quo* of functionalistic society.

Both logical positivism and linguistic philosophy have been revealed as definite methods of dealing with the present crisis-situation. Because they are controversial themselves, they cannot possibly assert that they have settled the crisis. All they can claim is that their method has presented different aspects of the world and of man's relation with the world. In this sense, they may be said to have developed different truth-perspectives. At best they can claim that their functionalistic approach is symptomatic of a functionalistic society, i.e., a society whose structure is determined by the scientific and technological way of production and style of living and that hopes to "solve" all conflict by the increasing satisfaction of man's material needs through the gradual extension of functional control and through operational thinking, i.e., improving the material conditions of its members in accordance with their specific circumstances. In this way, the social structure is kept intact and the *status quo* preserved.

In view of man's preoccupation with science and technology, the watchword of the pathology of philosophical language that was given out by linguistic philosophy assumes an ironical character. It becomes a case of the pot calling the kettle black. For surely the cult of science and technology, which is reflected in the cult of scientific language or the myth of ordinary language that is practised by logical positivism and linguistic philosophy respectively, is as pathological as was philosophy's attempt to comprehend the absolute by the systematic constitution of the world. This functionalistic approach of philosophy, too, has become an obsession, which explains the often fanatical attitude and almost religious fervour of some of its advocates. This obviously onesided alternative, which dissolves the world and man into a series of functional processes, in this way quantifying and levelling everything, cannot possibly be regarded as having settled the crisis by not accepting it as a crisis. It cannot be credited with having answered the question of the authentic character of human existence by having blended man with the functional processes of the world. This is so because it overlooks a most important thing, namely, the *qualitative* factor. This factor consists in man's being fundamentally different from material things; and it is precisely this qualitative distinction of man that causes the crisis to be natural and that defeats all attempts to overcome it by whatever method. This, however, will be discussed at a later stage. For the time being let it suffice to say that, as also Gellner has shown, the arbitrary handling of language by linguistic philosophy and its dogmatic insistence on playing the language game have given man the feeling of utter barrenness and frustration. The extreme functionalism of linguistic philosophy invites its own negation by rousing in man the desire for freedom from the *status quo*, the freedom of forming new ideas and concepts and of creating new values, which answer better than do the one-sided material values of the functionalistic society and the welfare state to man's real needs in his present situation. The fact that the demand for freedom from the *status quo* of the established functionalistic society is being made is already proof that the functionalistic method of dealing with the current crisis of truth has failed to meet man's real needs and to solve the problem of the authenticity of his existence.

Among others, the demand for freedom from the functionalistic alternative for dealing with the crisis as an alternative of the *status quo* has been made by Herbert Marcuse in his book *One-Dimensional Man*. It must, however, be kept in mind that Marcuse puts forward his demand in terms of his own alternative for dealing effectively with the present crisis. We certainly do not believe that his proposed alternative overcomes the crisis, as we hope to show at a later stage of our discussion, but we must concede that Marcuse's criticism of the functionalistic alternative as thinking in one dimension only, with the purpose of maintaining the *status quo*, i.e., the basic structure of the established functionalistic society, is indeed justifiable.

In regard to positivism and lingusitic philosophy, Marcuse points out the *conformist* nature of this kind of philosophy. He shows its ideological character as an instrument of subtle brainwashing, by which man is to be rendered incapable of thinking in terms of a dimension other than the functionalistic one. According to Marcuse, the so-called therapeutic method of positivism and linguistic philosophy leads to the levelling and crippling of man's thought, which makes him become the impotent tool of the forces that control the established functionalistic system. Naturally, the ideological character of linguistic analysis may not be prejudiced by connecting the struggle against the conceptual transcendence of the existing universe of language with the struggle against a political transcendence of the existing society, lest this ideological character should become obvious. But Marcuse implies that this connection exists, and he adds that linguistic analysis uses the language of the established functionalistic society with the aim of rendering harmless and ineffectual all real contradiction by including it in its system.

The first contradiction that is being overcome by the therapeutic method of linguistic analysis is, according to Marcuse, that between ordinary language and the language of philosophy. Thereby, however, the very motor of the development of human thought has been cut off. "In terms of the established universe," says Marcuse, "such contradicting modes of thought are negative thinking. 'The power of the negative' is the principle which governs the development of concepts, and contradiction becomes the distinguishing quality of Reason (Hegel)."[25] We have already observed that in logical positivism and in linguistic philosophy any qualitative distinction is denied and everything is described in terms of quantitative processes and measurable events. Thus Marcuse rightly points out that, in this sense, positivist thinking is a conformism both to the functionalistic method of the sciences and the functionalistic structure of society. Marcuse puts it as follows: "To the degree to which the given reality is scientifically comprehended and transformed, to the degree to which society becomes industrial and technological, positivism finds in the society the medium for the realization (and validation) of its concepts - harmony between theory and practice, truth and facts. Philosophic thought turns into affirmative thought; the philosophic critique criticizes *within* the societal framework and stigmatizes non-positive notions as mere speculation, dreams or fantasies."[26] In regard to contemporary linguistic philosophy, Marcuse discusses the mutilation of thinking by philosophy's own method with reference to J. L. Austin's contemptuous treatment of the alternative for the everyday use of words and with reference to Wittgenstein's demand that "philosophy should leave everything as it is." "At the later stage in contemporary positivism, it is no longer scientific and technical progress which motivates the repulsion (of the non-positive concepts); however, the contradiction of thought is no less severe because it is self-imposed – philosophy's own method."[27]

Marcuse shows that, by the separation of poetical and metaphysical language from everyday language in the form of grouping these various types of language under specific language games, the conflict between the language of philosophy and everyday language has been birdged and that everyday language is now represented as the only ligitimate

[25] *One-Dimensional Man*, p.171.
[26] *Op. cit.*, p. 172.
[27] *Op. cit.*, p. 173.

language which describes the world as it is, and in which, therefore, truth and reality fall together. With great perspicuity, however, Marcuse points out that even everyday language points beyond itself, namely, to the historical conditions in terms of which it is used. It points to an irrational factor over which man has no control. It becomes thus clear that the emergence in philosophical thinking of the functionalistic alternative for coping with the crisis of truth is in itself a historical process and, if seen in this way, points to other alternatives. It should also be borne in mind that the splitting off of the sciences (as the model of the functionalistic approach) from philosophy is such a historical process. It follows that philosophical thinking in general can never be one-dimensional, but is by nature multi-dimensional.

Marcuse reminds us of the difference between practical statements, such as "the broom stands in the corner" or "the taste of something like a pineapple" and concepts such as substance, idea, man, estrangement, freedom, government, England.[28] In accordance with its one-dimensional functionalistic method, linguistic philosophy equates the reality of the former with that of the latter. It is, however, not the task of ordinary thinking and ordinary language to describe the universe or else the relation between language and the world. On the other hand, philosophy is not concerned with the finding of brooms or the tasting of pineapple. The abstraction of experience by linguistic philosophy is justified only if it is really a matter of finding the broom and tasting the pineapple. "If it is a matter of finding the broom or tasting the pineapple, the abstraction is justified and the meaning can be ascertained and described without any transgression into the political universe. But in philosophy, the question is not that of finding the broom or tasting the pineapple - and even less so today should an empirical philosophy base itself on abstract experience. Nor is this abstractness corrected if linguistic analysis is applied to political terms and phrases. A whole branch of analytic philosophy is engaged in this undertaking, but the method already shuts off the concepts of a political, i.e., critical analysis. The operational or behavioral translation assimilates such terms as 'freedom,' 'government,' 'England,' with 'broom' and 'pineapple,' and the reality of the former with that of the latter."[29]

By translating everything into operational descriptions, the func-

---

[28] Marcuse points out that, in order to stress its distinction from conceptual philosophy and with the purpose of ridiculing it, linguistic philosophy is cynical in its studied use of banal sentences or "witty" ones, such as "the baldness of the present King of France".

[29] One-Dimensional Man, p. 181.

tionalistic alternative succeeds in retaining the *status quo*. But it does so at the expense of the authenticity of man's existence as an existence in freedom. The abstraction of experience and the bracketing of man's consciousness as a constitutive factor of the world leads to man's absorption into the metrical world of functional processes and thereby ends in man's estrangement from the world of concrete experience and, for this reason, in man's self-estrangement. For man is by nature he who constitutes the world in an ever new form, in accordance with the changing circumstances of life. And the functionalistic alternative is no exception to this. It should have become clear from our discussions that it, too, is man's conscious projection under particular historical circumstances. It, too, is only one possible perspective, which has been developed side by side with other perspectives as alternatives for coping with the present crisis of truth. As Ernest Gellner has shown, the functionalistic alternative for dealing with the problem of truth, just like any other philosophical alternative, has been developed by clearly recognizable underlying principles. This makes it a theory *about* language and *about* the world, no matter how categorically this fact is denied by the representatives of linguistic philosophy. But just because the representatives of the functionalistic alternative imagine themselves to be without any prejudice whatsoever, they cannot help being dogmatic and intolerant of other philosophical alternatives. The functionalistic alternative deprives man of the freedom of thought as the presupposition for bringing about a *qualitative* change and for the continual constitution of the world in a creative way, i.e., the continual recreation of culture and civilization in conformity with the changing conditions of life and man's outstanding needs, as they arise in the specific existential situation in which he finds himself.

Marcuse now argues that, in the present circumstances, man's greatest need consists in a need for freedom, i.e., the freedom to change the world in such a way that any kind of oppression as the result of the monopolistic way of production in the West and the state-monopolistic way of production in the East is removed by using science and technology not in the interests of the forces that are at present in control of production in the West and in the East, but in the interests of the whole. It is this alternative of the quantification of values that is unacceptable to us. We shall examine in detail this alternative and the implications it holds for man later on. For the time being, we agree with Marcuse when he says that the very artificial channelling of human thought by the functionalistic alternative points beyond this philosophical perspective and invites its own negation. We also see man's greatest need as the need for freedom in order that man should become conscious of his true nature and the authentic character of his existence, which, as a result of one-dimensional functionalistic thinking, has been suppressed. But in contradistinction to Marcuse, we do not believe that this need is exclusively materialistic in kind, nor do we believe that the authentic character of man's existence can be won by reading into the world and into history a dialectical principle. We are afraid that any constitution of the world and of history by the dialectical method leads to a new *theoretical conception* of the world and of man and thus to a new abstraction of human experience and, therefore, to new unauthenticity. Man's true freedom and real authentic existence can, in our opinion, not be conceived theoretically; they issue directly from our actual contingent experience. But before discussing these matters in greater detail, we shall first have to examine other alternatives that have been offered as a settlement of the present crisis of truth in order to establish in how far their claim to have resolved it is justifiable, if at all.

THE EXISTENTIAL ALTERNATIVE

It seems that the matter of this philosophical alternative for coping with the crisis of truth does not show the same uniformity as does the functionalistic alternative. This is the reason why we call it not the existentialist but the *existential* alternative. By this is meant the kind of philosophical thinking that takes its start from the phenomenon of human existence or, more accurately, from the phenomenon of man's *Dasein* (being-there). For whether one takes Heidegger's *Fundamental Ontology*, Jaspers's *Philosophy of Existence* or Sartre's *Existentialism*, to mention the three most outstanding representatives of the existential alternative for trying to overcome the crisis of truth, all three varieties of existential thinking have this in common that they start from man's *being-there*. Also, these three approaches within the existential alternative regard *anxiety* as their *Grundbefindlichkeit* (fundamental mood) or as their basic existential phenomenon of human existence.

The existential alternative may be said to link up with the phenomenological method (Husserl),[1] in as much as, in the existential approach, too, a *phenomenological reduction* takes place, because, like phenomenology, existential philosophy brackets the world of existing things. But in contradistinction to phenomenology, the step of *eidetic reduction* in existential thinking is not aimed at the analysis of conscious acts as *intentional acts*, which include the world of existing things or *das Seiende* in the form of transcendental *noema*. Existential philosophy does not seek to establish the meaning or essence of the transcendental *noema*, but there *eidetic reduction* (if it is permissible to use this term in connection with existential thought) may be said to aim at an analysis of man's being-there or else of the various existen-

---

[1] For a detailed investigation of the phenomenological method, including existential philosophy, cf. H. Spiegelberg, *The Phenomenological Movement*.

tials (e.g., being-in-the-world, anxiety, care, border-situations, death, to mention a few phenomena of being-there at random) that emerge from the basic phenomenon of being-there. This fundamental phenomenon is conceived from man's basic experience of finding himself thrown into a foreign, hostile world, which rouses in him the feeling that, in his thinking and acting, he is entirely thrown upon himself. Because man feels that he is thrown into the nothing, anxiety, as the expression of the nothing, is regarded by the existential approach as man's basic experience, no matter how existential thinkers see it and how they differ in regard to other existentials or phenomena of being-there. With Jaspers, for instance, the elucidation of the forms of existential consciousness are: Existence as a self, anxiety, loneliness, self-deification, play, shame, awareness of historicity, the border-situations, communication with others, love, the possibility of achieving a break-through to the absolute (freedom).[2] With Heidegger, the most important existentials are: Existence as being-to-death, being-in-the-world, anxiety, care (Sorge), understanding, being-in-a-mood (Gestimmtheit), being-thrown-into-the-world (Geworfenheit). With Sartre, we get the following outstanding existentials: Existence as *actualitas*, i.e., as man's projecting himself into the world from the nothing, anxiety, being-by-itself (*pour-soi*), being-seen (communication), freedom-to-the-nothing.

The various existential approaches have that in common that they, in accordance with their respective interpretation of the phenomenon of human existence or man's being-there as a direct basic experience and their respective elucidation of the existentials, seek to master the current crisis of truth by penetrating to what they regard as man's authentic existence. The chief cause of the development of the existential alternative for dealing with the present crisis of truth may well be traced to man's self-estrangement as a result of the *Cogito, ergo sum* thinking of Descartes and especially of Hegel on the one hand (which led to the identification of thinking and being) and positivistic scientism on the other (which dissolves man's self into a set of functional relations). Both these *ids* or anonyma, the idealist and the scientific one, proved a menace to man's concrete individual existence, and this menace became

---

[2] In the last paragraph of his work *Philosophie* entitled: "Ruhe in der Wirklichkeit", which is found in vol.III, Jaspers makes it quite clear that anxiety is the condition for the jump to tranquility and thus for the experience of being in failure. In order to accomplish this jump, anxiety must cease to regard itself as the last in the face of the uncertainty of our existence. It must realize that it points beyond itself and so accomplish the jump to peace. Jaspers says: "Es ist das Grundfaktum unserer Existenz im Dasein, dass die Wirklichkeit, die die vernichtende Angst hervorbringt, weder ohne Angst gesehen werden kann, wie sie eigentlich ist, noch ohne den Übergang der Angst in Ruhe."

very real during the two World Wars. These two great conflagrations were nothing but the coming to a head of a crisis that had been latent for a long time before it came out into the open, a crisis that had been brought about by the absolutization of idealist thought on the one hand and of the sciences and technology on the other. The shock to man was so great and the existential dilemma into which these forces had plunged him was so exasperating, that he lost confidence in both of them and became very sceptical in constitutive metaphysics on the one hand and of science and technology on the other.

The apocalyptical feeling that was aroused in man as a result of the invention of the atom bomb and that grew in proportion to the further development of deadly nuclear weapons steeped mankind in despair and anxiety. Small wonder, then, if anxiety came to be regarded as man's fundamental experience by the existential thinkers. This experience was the manifestation of the nothing by which man found himself sourrounded after the old concepts of truth, being, goodness and beauty had finally expired under the shells and bombs of the World Wars. The experience of anxiety revealed to man his self-estrangement and alienation from the world. It roused in him the need to re-examine the nature of his existence in the world and to reassess the relation in which he stood with the world. In other words, man, again, from the new existential situation in which he found himself, asked the old question about the authenticity of his existence. This time he attempted to answer this question not by starting from the world and by deriving the authentic nature of his existence from the theoretical constitution of the world by either idealist metaphysics or the sciences, but by starting from his very being-there. It can thus be seen that existential philosophy moved very much into the centre the question about freedom. Anxiety, as man's fundamental experience, had a purging effect. It is true that it caused man to suffer and to despair, but at the same time it set him free from the fetters of convention, from traditional cultural and moral values. This experience led to a new orientation on the part of man and opened new channels to him for gaining access to being (see footnote 2). The experience of anxiety is of a transcendent nature, it may be regarded as the gateway to being.

This new being, however, is no longer a world that man constitutes in his mind metaphysically (as was done by idealist metaphysics) or scientifically (as was the case with positivist philosophy). Existential philosophy finds being in man's very being-there. With Jaspers, being or the absolute is symbolized in the form of ciphers and is experienced in the border situations of life, which reveal man's failure to embrace the absolute. With Heidegger, the absolute is experienced in man's being-there as a being-to-death. As such it "ek-sists" as the *Lichtung des Seins* (clearance or manifestation of being). With Sartre, the absolute manifests itself as the absolute freedom man experiences by the negating power of his consciousness in its relation with the things of the world, by which man is plunged into the nothing.

It thus becomes evident that the existential alternative for coping with the crisis of truth rejects classical metaphysics (i.e., the constitution of the absolute from the world of existing things), but it likewise rejects science and positivist philosophy as a means of working out the authentic character of human existence. The reason for rejecting positivist philosophy in this regard is that the functionalistic, metrical nature of its method has a levelling effect. In the sciences and in positivist philosophy, man is subjected to the same methodological procedure as is any material object of the world, say, for instance, a stone. By the functionalistic method of the sciences and of positivist philosophy, man is blended with what Heidegger calls the *Man*, i.e., the impersonal metrical world of quantification or the mass. We have already discussed the Third Person approach in regard to logical positivism and linguistic philosophy. In order to separate clearly the field of philosophy from the province of the sciences, Jaspers, for example, holds that philosophical world orientation leads to the clear separation of the multiple objects in space and time as *Objektsein* (object-being), the exploration of which is the task of the individual sciences, from being in the form of human existence, the exploration of which is the task of philosophy. It may also be said that the proper task of philosophy is to analyze the phenomenon of being-there (Dasein) in its search of being (Sein). This is what Jaspers calls *Existenzerhellung* (elucidation of existence, i.e., man's individual existence). *Existenzerhellung*, however, is not understood by Jaspers as a *Fundamental Ontology* (as is Heidegger's philosophy of human existence), but as an elucidation of the states of existential consciousness, i.e., the existentials which we mentioned previously. *Existenzerhellung* makes possible for us the *Sprung zur Transzendenz* (the jump from our finite existential experience to the transcendent). Sartre has stated most clearly that existence is prior to essence and not the other way around.[3] For Sartre, human existence is always an existence-in-freedom, in as much as human consciousness is always a

---

[3] In this regard, cf. "L'existentialisme est un humanisme", in German in: *Jean-Paul Sartre, Drei Essays*, ed. by W. Schmiele, paragraph entitled: "Der atheistische Existentialismus".

pour-soi and can never become one with the *en-soi* (i.e., man can never exist like a material thing, but always remains a foreigner in this world, or, as Sartre sometimes says, a god that turned out to be a failure). It follows that, according to Sartre as well, the sciences will not reveal the authentic nature of man's existence.

The existential approach has that in common with the functionalistic alternative for coping with the crisis of truth that for it, too, the metaphysical or the absolute is unknowable. Jaspers, as a Kantian philosopher, advocates the idea of a *Spiel der Metaphysik*.[4] That is to say, there are many ways and possibilities of experiencing the absolute in various border-situations. And there are many kinds of ciphers in terms of which the absolute is represented. This reminds us of Kant's *noumena* as being of regulative significance for our practical life. All in all, Jaspers reduces metaphysics to metaphysical experience in our being-there. It is in this that the existential alternative for dealing with the crisis of truth differs radically from the functionalistic alternative. The two philosophical approaches to the problem of truth, therefore, are diametrically opposed to one another.

After discussing the existential alternative in general, we shall now examine in greater detail Heidegger's philosophy, i.e., his particular method of dealing with the crisis of truth. We shall do so with a view to establishing how he proposes to overcome this crisis and whether he succeeds in doing so.

Heidegger does not wish to be labelled an existentialist. He rejects Sartre's fundamental thesis that existence is prior to essence when he says: "Der Hauptsatz von Sartre über den Vorrang der existentia vor der essentia rechtfertigt indessen den Namen 'Existentialismus' als einen dieser Philosophie gemässen Titel. Aber der Hauptsatz des 'Existentialismus' hat mit jenem Satz in 'Sein und Zeit' nicht das geringste gemeinsam, abgesehen davon, dass in 'Sein und Zeit' ein Satz über das Verhältnis von essentia und existentia noch gar nicht ausgesprochen werden kann, denn es gilt dort, ein Vorläufiges vorzubereiten".[5] From this it becomes clear that Heidegger regards *Sein und Zeit* as a preliminary work to another major work which he intended to write, but which, for some reason or other, he did not write. Instead of a major work that would be a complement of *Sein und Zeit*, there appeared a number of essays, in which Heidegger performs the famous *Kehre* or turn-about in his thinking, which puzzled so many philosophers. Heidegger stresses

---

4 Cf. *Philosophie*, vol. III, pp. 33–34.
5 *Über den Humanismus*, p. 18.

that "Diese Kehre ist nicht eine Änderung des Standpunkts von 'Sein und Zeit', sondern in ihr gelangt das versuchte Denken erst in die Ort-schaft der Dimension, aus der 'Sein und Zeit' erfahren ist und zwar aus der Grunderfahrung der Seinsvergessenheit".[6] In other words, the *Kehre* means that Heidegger's philosophy comprises two phases, (i) the metaphysics of being-there (ii) being-there as *Wurf des Seins* or the projection of being. In the first phase, man's being-there is experienced as a being-to-nothing or a being-to-death. This phase, which is trea-ted in Heidegger's chief work *Sein und Zeit*, is the stage of *Seinsverges-senheit* (forgetfulness of being). At that stage, man feels that he is thrown into the nothing and that he is himself nothing, i.e., condemned to die. It is the phenomenological stage, which Jaspers calls *Existenzerhellung*. At that stage, man becomes acutely aware of the change, the periodicity and the historicity of his existence as well as of the termination of his existence by death in the future. It is through the *Grundbefindlichkeit* (fundamental feeling or mood) of anxiety that man's *Sorge* (care) is aroused. These two fundamental feelings, anxiety and care, draw man's attention to himself, to his own individual existence. They drive him to ask the questions: Who am I? What is my purpose? And as the ans-wer is obviously: I am historicity, temporality and finiteness; my ex-istence is anchored in death and fulfilled in death, man feels called upon to take up a heroic stand to live up to the challenge of the time and to accept himself as what he really is, a being-to death. Heidegger says: "Das eigentliche Sein zum Tode, d.h. die Endlichkeit der Zeitlichkeit, ist der verborgene Grund der Geschichtlichkeit des Daseins."[7] Heideg-ger's thinking is a philosophy of personal engagement or of *existential facticity*, i.e., man's self-determination and self-creation in the face of nothing and of death. It is that which Heidegger understands by *Ge-schichte*. It is not history in the sense of that which is passed, but it is acting in conformity with actual occurrence or *Geschehen*, i.e., in accord-ance with the fact that my very being-there is temporal, historical and therefore an event. "Geschichte als Geschehen," says Heidegger, "ist das aus der Zukunft bestimmte, das Gewesene übernehmende Hin-durchhandeln und Hindurchleiden durch die Gegenwart."[8] In accor-dance with this, Heidegger defines philosopy in *Sein und Zeit* as follows: "Philosophie ist universal phänomenologische Ontologie, ausgehend von der Hermeneutik des Daseins, die als Analytik der Existenz das

[6] *Über den Humanismus*, p.17.
[7] *Sein und Zeit*, p. 386.
[8] *Einführung in die Metaphysik*, p.34.

Ende des Leitfadens alles philosophischen Fragens dort festgemacht hat, woraus es entspringt und wohin es zurückschlägt."[9]

It is now by this heroic attitude of the *dennoch*, the nevertheless, which he takes up in the face of the nothing and the face of death that man arrives at a new understanding of being. He begins to realize that the question about being is meaningful only if it is asked from his being-there. W. Schulz points out that, in order to realize the necessity of Heidegger's *Fundamental Ontology*, it becomes necessary to ask the question about the meaning of being again, in the face of the having become questionable of the old ontology. This, says Schulz, "leistet bereits der erste Teil von 'Sein und Zeit'. Er (Heidegger) treibt die leitende Frage nach der Ganzheit des Daseins so weit vor, dass sich die Zeit als der Sinn von Sein zeigt, d.h. als das Woraufhin des primären Entwurfs, aus dem Dasein schon immer existierend in seiner Möglichkeit begriffen werden kann."[10] Being may thus be said to reveal itself in the temporal character of man's being-there; for it is in this that the ontic structure of man's being-there consists.

As man now is the only one among all the other existents of the world who is able to ask the question about being, Heidegger holds that man is predestined by being to do so and that asking this question is the purpose of his life. "Das Fragen dieser Frage ist als Seinsmodus eines Seienden selbst von dem her wesenhaft bestimmt, wonach in ihm gefragt ist - vom Sein. Dieses Seiende, das wir selbst sind und das unter anderem die Seinsmöglichkeit des Fragens hat, fassen wir terminologisch als Dasein. Die ausdrückliche und durchsichtige Fragestellung nach dem Sinn von Sein verlangt vorgängige Explikation eines Seienden (Dasein) hinsichtlich seines Seins."[11]

This passage at the beginning of *Sein und Zeit* already points to the reversal of thinking that must take place after the analysis of our being-there and the discovery of it as transcendence into the nothing. If the tradition of metaphysical thinking (the constitution of the absolute from the world) is abandoed and if the nothing is not objectified and absolutized itself, then the nothing becomes being, which is incomprehensible to us and which is present in our being-there.[12] The reversal of thinking, now, consists in looking at human existence no longer from the point of view of a *Seiende*, i.e., a periodical, finite existent,

---

[9] P.38.
[10] "Über den philosophiegeschichtlichen Ort Martin Heideggers," in: *Philosophische Rundschau.*
[11] *Sein und Zeit*, p. 7.
[12] In this regard, cf. M. Heidegger, *Was ist Metaphysik?*.

but from the point of view of concealed being, of which man no longer disposes by rational conception, but which disposes of him and manifests itself in his being-there. Whereas, therefore, in *Sein und Zeit* historical time was regarded as having its origin in the event of final being-there, it is seen now as having its ground in non-existing being.[13] Heidegger himself called his change of view-point in regard to being-there "Das Denken der Kehre von Sein und Zeit zu Zeit und Sein."[14]

Heidegger's being-there as a mode or a projection of being justifies his claim that his philosophy is neither a Philosophy of Existence nor an Existentialism, but a *Fundamental Ontology*. In both cases that of Jaspers and that of Sartre being-there *insists* in the world and being is experienced either in its negation of being-there,i.e., in man's failure to embrace it (Jaspers), or in the nausea or repulsion I feel in the face of the dull, unreasonable and impenetrable objects, an aversion which drives me into the nothing (Sartre). With Heidegger, on the other hand, being *ek-sists*, i.e., stands out into the nothing as the *Lichtung des Seins* or the clearance of being. Heidegger can thus point out that, from the very start, he uses "existence" in an entirely different way from the manner in which Sartre uses it. Heidegger uses "existence" in the sense of *svbstance*, i.e., in the sense of *ek-sistene*, which is regarded as being-there in historical time at first, and as an event of being later. While Sartre's existence is *epistemological* or *phenomenological* and refers to *actualitas* in contradistinction to mere possibility or idea, Heidegger's *ek-sistence* is *ontological* and names the part man plays or the task he performs *im Geschick der Wahrheit*, i.e., according to the destiny imposed upon him by truth.

It is important to note that, in accordance with this view of man's being-there as *ek-sistence*, man no longer disposes of being, but being disposes of him. As a projection of being, he is thrown into the world and sticks out into the nothing. But he often forgets this and seeks to constitute being from the world, thereby arriving at the nothing. The result is that, by his *Seinsvergessenheit* or forgetfulness of being, man is unhoused or deprived of his authentic abode and lives in a *Weltnacht* or a world-night. The crisis (world dilemma) and the darkness in which he finds himself as a result of his forgetfulness of being can be overcome only if he becomes conscious again of his true abode. In other words, he must cease to constitute being himself. This will only plunge him into the nothing and will end in self-estrangement. Man will re-

---

[13] In this connection, cf. Löwith, *Heidegger, Denker in dürftiger Zeit*, ch. II, p.43.
[14] *Über den Humanismus*, p.17.

cover the authentic nature of his existence only if he realizes the impossibility of embracing being by cheating time, i.e., by attempting to overcome his own temporality and historicity in constituting an absolute in eternal time, such as Hegel's absolute spirit, for example. Such an attempt will only lead to the revenge of time, i.e., the termination or calling in question of his own constitution by another.[15] Man must therefore accept the historical part which has been thrust upon him by being, his *Seinsgeschick*.[16] He must become aware that as *Platzhalter des Nichts*, the occupant of the nothing, he is at the same time the *Hüter des Seins*, the guardian of being, in which he dwells. The abode of being is language, by which man says *Das Diktat der Wahrheit des Seins*, i.e., the dictation of the truth of being. That is what Heidegger understands by thinking, in which being communicates itself to man as an event. This communication of being in thinking is thus historical. Its history is already told when thinkers express it.[17]

If man is embedded in being and if thinking is really the saying of the dictation of the truth of being, it follows that man can as little philosophize *about* being, as man, in the case of Wittgenstein, was able to philosophize about the world in which he was regarded as being embedded and which he was stating in meaningful propositions. In other words, just as, with Wittgenstein, the wholeness of the world remained a mystery, with Heidegger the wholeness of being remained concealed to man.

It is true that "Das Denken geleitet die geschichtliche Ek-sistenz, d.h. die humanitas des homo humanus, in den Bereich des Aufgangs des Heilen,"[18] but, together with the whole, there appears, in the clearance of being, *evil*, which does not take its origin in human action, but in the *Bösartige des Grimmes* (the maliciousness of the grim). Both the whole and the grim can be present in being because, on account of its being concealed, it is controversial. It thus becomes clear that the *Nichten des Nichts* i.e., the nothing of the nothing, takes its origin in being itself and manifests itself in the *Lichtung des Seins* or the clearance of being, i.e., in man's being-there, as the *Nichthafte*, or the nothinglike.[19]

---

[15] In this regard,cf. Heidegger's essay, "Wer ist Nietzsche's Zarathustra", in: *Vorträge und Aufsätze*.

[16] Cf. Friedrich Nietzsche's doctrine of "amor fati".

[17] Cf. M. Heidegger, *Über den Humanismus*, also "Was heisst Denken" in: *Vorträge und Aufsätze*.

[18] *Über den Humanismus*, p.43.

[19] Although we followed here mostly Heidegger's essay *Über den Humanismus*, these ideas of Heidegger's are also found in many variations in his essays contained in *Vorträge und Aufsätze*.

Language and its modality, thinking, are therefore not instruments of man at all, but his home, which is provided for him by being. It is not man that, through language and thinking, advances towards being and truth, but it is the absolute that, through language and thinking, advances towards man. By taking up the right attitude, i.e., by being in expectation of being and accepting himself as temporality and becoming, man should get being to talk to him. What matters, therefore, is to take up a new attitude towards being. This new attitude will make man abandon all attempts to overcome finiteness, periodicity and change by metaphysical constitution, or to fuse man with the world by dissolving his consciousness into a set of functional or propositional relations. By setting him free from the world and by referring him to his own being-there as a projection of being, Heidegger gives man the idea that he should always be on the way to being; he should always keep himself open to it, instead of evading the issue by the conception of his own world and taking refuge in it, be it the world of metaphysics or the world of science.

The *Aufbruch zum Sein*, i.e., the setting out on the way to being, is the task that has been set to man. The realization of this task, hopes Heidegger, will make man take up a new attitude towards life and his fellowman. In so doing, he would recover the authentic nature of his existence and his freedom of action. If Wittgenstein sought to overcome the crisis by the therapeutic method in regard to our language, i.e., by merely letting language state the facts of the world or, later, by conceiving common language as describing the world in terms of language games, Heidegger attempted to settle the crisis by letting language say the truth of being. It needs little reflection to realize that, in contradistinction to Wittgenstein, it is not the functionalistic aspect of language in which Heidegger is interested, but rather the metaphoric aspect of language. Small wonder, then, that Heidegger regards poetic language as the most suitable kind of language to give expression to the multidemensional character of being. The poetry which he appreciates most in this respect is that of the German poet Hölderlin.[20]

It is obvious that Heidegger tries to overcome the acute crisis man is at present experiencing as a crisis of truth by getting man re-housed in being. But this re-housing takes place not by the constitution of

---

[20] Cf.M.Heideggers, *Erläuteringen zu Hölderlins Dichtungen*, also cf. "Was heisst Denken?" in: *Vorträge und Aufsätze*, where Heidegger, with reference to Hölderlin, says that the nature of poetry consists in thinking. Although Heidegger distinguishes between that which is said by poetry and that which is said in the ordinary way of thinking, he points out that both kinds of saying may express the same thing.

being from the *Seiende*, i.e., the existing world, but by getting man to re-think the nature of the relation of his existence with the world as one of permanent change, periodicity and temporality, into which he cannot escape through scientific constitution or analysis merely for the sake of refuge. Man's re-housing takes place by getting him to accept himself as that which he really is, a being-to-nothing or a being-to-death. In so doing, he will recover the authentic character of his existence. It is by taking this heroic or defiant stand in the midst of change, finiteness, perishability and nothingness that man, eventually, comes to see his existence as *ek-sistence*, that is to say, as the manifestation of being, the truth of which he alone is able to say and the guardian of which he is. By conceiving himself as the *substance of being*, man takes up an heroic attitude towards life, which reminds us of Friedrich Nietzsche's revaluation of all values. By his heroism and his resolution to be in the face of nothingness, by which he is surrounded and which manifests itself in his being-there, in as much as he is a being-to-death, man rises above the anxiety, despair and frustration, by which he was ruled before. By finding his dwelling in being, man deprives death of its sting. It is nothing hostile anymore, something which is feared, but, on the contrary, it becomes the natural and crowning event in human life. It becomes the very ground of man's being-there and manifests itself in the finiteness, temporality and historicity of human existence. It determines the ontic structure of being-there as a whole, as that in which being is present. It creates for man the possibility to be and to lead an authentic existence.[21]

In switching his thinking from existence to *ek-sistence*, thus performing the famous *Kehre*, Heidegger becomes the anti-thinker to classical metaphysics (Hegel) as well as to transcendental philosophy (Husserl). In both approaches the absolute is constituted from the world as the absolute spirit (Hegel) or transcendental consciousness (Husserl) and as such is regarded as the *real ground* of the world. In this way, the absolute becomes the subject that constitutes itself. At this act of self-constitution on the part of the absolute, we experience at the same time our finiteness and our limitation. Heidegger, now, from the finiteness of the *Faktizität*, i.e., the constitutive act of the subject, draws the conclusion that we cannot place ourselves outside this *Faktizität*. In other words, as man is himself inside this constitutive act, it is impossible for

---

[21] In regard to Heidegger's analysis of death as the determining factor of human existence, which refers man's being-there to its own possibility to be, cf. the second part of *Sein und Zeit*.

him to constitute the absolute from the finite, existing world of which he is a part, because, in so doing, he remains himself in this world. We have already observed that, if man does attempt to constitute the absolute from the finite world, he arrives at the nothing. Hence, being cannot be constituted by him at all, but can only be *experienced* in man's very being-there. This is so because man is embedded in being, which he experiences as not-being, finiteness, becoming, being-to-death, anxiety and care. He is *in das Nichts hinein gehalten*, i.e., projected by being into the nothing. As the *Platzhalter des Nichts* or the occupant of the nothing, he is the *Hüter des Seins* or the guardian of being. Being is *insistent*, which means it stands into man; being-there is *ek-sistent*, which means it stands out into the nothing as the *Lichtung des Seins*, i.e., the clearance of being or the manisfestation of being in man's very being-there.

Now, man no longer disposes of the absolute or the whole as was the case in classical metaphysics. He no longer controls it and causes it to become finite by constituting it as a subject. In fact, the opposite is the case. The absolute disposes of man, in that he experiences it in his being-there as not-being. In his impotence, man feels that he is embedded in the absolute or the whole, which he sees, so to speak, through the veil of not-being. For this reason, the absolute is no longer knowable or comprehensible. We can no longer form a concept of it, such as Hegel's absolute spirit, for example. According to Heidegger, the metaphysical is experiental as man dwells in it. It is thus above all the poet who can say the whole. In this sense, language is the abode of being.

From this it should become clear that Heidegger's starting-point in dealing with the crisis of truth is the exact opposite of that of Wittgenstein. While Wittgenstein in "solving" the conflict between man and the world, subject and object, brackets the subject (i.e., man's consciousness) and treats language as stating the events of the world in propositions, Heidegger brackets the object (i.e., the world of existing things) and treats language as saying the dictation of the truth of being. Neither philosopher can thus think an absolute as a self-constituting subject, because man cannot step outside the world. According to Wittgenstein, therefore, man leads a meaningful existence only as long as he simply records his experience of the world and abstains from asking unanswerable questions about the world. According to Heidegger, man leads an authentic existence only if he follows his experience of being as it manifests itself in his being-there, which finds expression especially in poetic language, and if he refrains from constituting being as the absolute from the world.

Wittgenstein and Heidegger have that in common that they both refrain from constituting the world as a metaphysical subject and that they both wish to record their immediate experience. But by bracketing the subject and treating language as an "objective" instrument of recording this experience in a meaningful way, Wittgenstein fuses language (and thus man) with natural events. In this way, propositions become the truth-functions of the world, and the functional relations in which they stand with one another, so to speak, represent the substance of the world. Wittgenstein, therefore, seeks to set man free by curing him of his metaphysical pathology of asking questions about the world and by fusing him with the world. Heidegger does the opposite. By bracketing the world, he leads man out of his self-estrangement into which science and for that matter positivist philosophy had driven him. In so doing, he leads man to his being-there, in which he experiences being and is enabled to lead an authentic life, i.e., living up to his real nature as a being-to-nothing or a being-to-death. It is by taking a resolution to be in the face of nothing and to death that man is free. It is this which Heidegger designates as "Freiheit zum Tode"[22]. Being, according to Heidegger, is insistent in man's existence, and because this is so, man comes to understand himself as the *ek-sistence* of being, in which he dwells and with which, for this reason, he is fused.

By comparing Heidegger's approach with that of Wittgenstein, we have become aware of how the former attempted to overcome the crisis of truth, which man came to experience with particular vehemence in consequence of the two World Wars. While Wittgenstein's alternative may be said to seek to overcome it by blending man's thinking (and for that matter philosophy) entirely with the functional and operational relationalism of the sciences and technology, Heidegger's alternative may be regarded as attempting to master the crisis by reducing man's thinking (and thus philosophy) to giving expression to being in the arts, especially in poetry. We have already witnessed in regard to the functionalistic alternative for coping with the crisis of truth that the arbitrary nature of its therapeutic method is nothing else but another form of the constitution of the world by man under specific historical circumstances. As such, it is controversial and is called in question by other alternatives that are offered for the purpose of dealing with the crisis. Heidegger's alternative, too, suffers from the same defects. As the constitution of man's metaphysical experience in philosophical terms, it forms a counter-project to Wittgenstein's re-

[22] *Sein und Zeit*, p. 266.

cording of man's experience of the world in terms of propositional relations. But as such, it reveals one of man's needs which had been neglected
by the functionalistic alternative, namely, the need of giving expression
to his experience of the irrational in terms of artistic symbols and meta-
phors. The "objective" functionalization of this kind of experience by
contemporary linguistic philosophy, i.e., its mere description in terms
of language games, cannot possibly give satisfaction to man's need to give
spontaneous expression to it. The merit of Heidegger's existential approach consists in having shown the reality of the irrational as opposed
to the rational and the important part the irrational plays in human life.
Fritz Heinemann states it as follows: "Heidegger is quite right, the ontological problem of not-being cannot be reduced to a merely linguistic or
logical problem. It may be possible to get rid of such propositions as
'Pegasus is not' with the help of Russel's theory of descriptions but the
hard fact of death remains and cannot be eliminated by the most sophisti-
cated linguistic analysis."[23] That Heidegger's truth-perspective is not
the whole truth is shown by the great amount of criticism it has provoked
and by the philosophical alternatives that were offered in order to re-
medy its defects and shortcomings. Thus Fritz Heinemann in *Existentialism and the Modern Predicament* calls in question Heidegger's
philosophy by pointing to the uncritical assumption by Heidegger of
an underlying absolute. He further tries to show that cutting off the
natura naturans from the *natura naturata* by the existential approach
in general (i.e., the bracketing of the world in the case of Heidegger)
makes true communication impossible and causes man to turn against
himself, i.e., to see himself as nothing. It could thus be said that Sartre's
thesis that, as a source of negation, man is nothing and is condemned
to be free in the sense of being a *pour-soi* in contradistinction to the
en-soi of the objects (which man strives to become in vain, but cannot,
so that he feels nauseated at the obstrusiveness of dull, determined
matter and regards the nothing as his deliverance from an unbearable
nightmare) is the consistent outcome of the existential alternative.
Fritz-Joachim von Rintelen regards man's existential self-creation in the
face of nothing as a mere dynamic act or gesture, as a permanent being-
on-the-way, bare of any real content or of any binding norms and values. Von Rintelen regards norms and values as essential for any true
philosophy. He points to the dangers that are concealed in the extreme
dynamism of existential philosophy where action is regarded as the
highest value: "Wir könnten von dem allein selig machenden Willen

[23] *Existenlialism and the Modern Predicament*, p. 98.

oder der allein selig machenden Tätigkeit als solcher sprechen. Nur sie sei sinvoll (s. in etwa Sorge als Sinn)...Was aber wird nicht alles möglich, *wenn nicht* dem Tun bindende Wertgebungen vorgelagert sind. Dass müsste nach den Erlebnissen der letzten Zeit heute um so einhelliger von uns eingesehen werden."[24] In terms of the two contradictory alternatives for coping with the present crisis or truth, von Rintelen would seek their reconciliation by trying to restore the medieval unity of life and spirit, eros and logos. According to von Rintelen, man's suffering is due to the loss of balance and a split of man's personality by man's giving himself over to an impulse, a chaotic vitalisma, as it finds expression in the philosophy of life (in a wide sense, including existential thinking) on the one hand and to a degenerated formal intellectualism (as in neo-positivist philosophy) on the other. In regard to Heidegger, von Rintelen asks: "Kann hier die heutige Weltnacht, die Entfremdung von aller Ursprünglichkeit, wie Heidegger sagt, sicher durchschritten werden? Ist hier ein wirklicher Durchbruch, ein Ansatz dazu gelungen? Sind doch viele von uns durch diese Philosophie und ihre beschwörend klingende Sprache im tiefsten aufgerüttelt und zu neuer Bereitschaft aufgerufen. Oder ist hierdurch das Vergänglichkeitsbewusstsein ohne jeden darüber hinausführenden Blick nicht erst vollends offenbar geworden, entscheidender noch als im Positivismus und Materialismus, da dieses Denken tiefer herabschichtet?"

The self-sufficiency of man's being-there, man's exposure to the nothing and his self-creation in the face of nothing required of him a heroic act of *Entschlossenheit* (i.e., being resolved to accept himself as that which he really is, a being-to-nothing or a being-to-death, so keeping himself open for the future) to live up to his destiny as a historical being and, in so doing, to set out on the way towards the future. There was thus no settling down in a self-constituted world, but there was a constant being-on-the-way. This holds also true when Heidegger sees man's existence as the *ek-sistence* of being, because the latter is concealed. There are times when being withdraws from man. Thus man is forever called upon to listen to the dictation of the truth of being. He must forever be on the alert lest he should become the victim of an illusion which he takes for the truth, thus moving on a *Holzweg* or a false path, which leads him away from his authentic existence into an illusory world of unauthenticity.[25]

---

[24] *Philosophie der Endlichkeit*, p. 139.
[25] In connection with this, cf. *Was ist Metaphysik* and *Holzwege*. Metaphysics is no longer

It is obvious that (to use the title of Karl Löwith's work on Heidegger's thinking) Heidegger is a *Denker in dürftiger Zeit*, i.e., a thinker in a time without imposing metaphysical systems, without a coherent world-view and without binding norms and values. As Gerhard Krüger would say in his work *Grundfragen der Philosophie:* The subject (man) has dissociated himself more and more from the object (nature) and, in so doing, has come to posit himself against an object. In the course of this process of dissociation from nature an increasing functionalization of the subject took place, so that, to-day, the subject has become a mere fleeting event among other fleeting events. It is this that Gerhard Krüger called die *Vergeschichtlichung des Ichs*, which reaches its climax in existential philosophy. In view of the fact that the self was either dissolved into a set of functional propositional relations by positivist philosophy or was reduced to a mere historical act by existential philosophy makes it understandable that there developed among men a growing need for greater security, a need for some firmer ground, on which man would feel he was borne, a need for some brighter outlook on life, which would give man new confidence and new hope.

It is now, above all, Otto Friedrich Bollnow, who, especially in his chief-work *Neue Geborgenheit*, pointed out the *positive* experiences of human life, such as joy, happiness, contentment and peace, for example, in contradistinction to Heidegger's fundamental experiences of anxiety and of care as a result of man's exposure to the nothing. Bollnow has shown that the existential virtues of defiant heroism, firm resolution and constant readiness must be complemented by virtues such as confidence, hope, patience and gratitude. These latter values carry man, so to speak, in the midst of all change, becoming, historicity and finiteness and provide him with a firm basis. For Bollnow, man, in his being-there, is not merely a passive, suffering and experiencing being, but rather an active and creative one. There are not only times of crisis, but there are quiet times as well. The previously mentioned carrying values have ontological as well as ethical significance. They point towards a transcendent world, which we cannot know, and they manifest themselves in human action, planning and building. They reveal man's hope in time (hope for the future) and his dwelling in space.[26] These

conceived as the constitution of the world by an absolute subject, but it now becomes metaphysical experience in man's being-there. The metaphysics from Descartes to Hegel is reinterpreted as an error, which has its origin not in human deficiency, but which is, "zugeschicktes Geschick". In this respect, also cf. W. Schulz "Über den philosophiegeschichtlichen Ort Heideggers", in: *Philosopische Rundschau.*

[26] In this respect, cf. O. F. Bollnow *Mensch und Raum.*

values also manifest themselves in our relations with our fellowman as, for instance, confidence, which Bollnow regards as a mode of hope. The experience of confidence moves my fellowman into my immediate presence through love.[27] When man is in a festive mood and when he is dancing as well, the joy and delight he experiences connect him with the carrying ground of his life and his existence. The transcendent character of the positive values becomes clear when we realize that they point to something that exists outside us or something that will happen in the future and that fills us with happy expectation. These values even point to another world, e.g., when, in the moment of ecstatic joy and happy self-abandonment, finite time is transcended. In this short-lived experience, man is linked with the eternal.

By this is shown that the above-mentioned carrying values are counterbalances to the nothing and to the negative experiences of anxiety and care in existential philosophy. They are complementary to the one-sided heroic virtues of bravery, resolution and readiness of existential philosophy. They convert its pessimism and gloomy outlook into optimism and gay expectation. The future is not only steeped in the shadow of death, but it also holds great promises and is full of anticipation. It is these that really determine our life, our action and our planning, death being outside our actual experience. The absolute is not experienced as mere negativity, but we experience it in our creative acts and in our composure, even if it is true that, over and over again, we have to defend against the nothing, which constantly threatens to devour it, the home we build for ourselves (our various human truths and cultural systems that we keep constructing throughout history) and so must always be on the alert.[28] Even if we are finite and historical beings, we remain orientated towards the transcendent through our hope, confidence and belief, and, occasionally, we experience the transcendent in the ecstasy of joy and happiness and in the peace of our content.

We observe how Bollnow links up man with the world again. Man is no longer thrown into the world as a stranger, but he is in the world as an active creative being. It is as such that he experiences the whole and the healthy, and it is this very experience that points to the trans-

---

[27] In this connection, cf. Gabriel Marcel, *Le Mystère de l'Etre*.
Bollnow wrote an article on Marcel's mystery of being, which appeared in *Französischer Existentialismus*, ch. VIII, pp. 149–166.
[28] In this regard, cf. De Saint-Exupéry, *Citadelle*, as well as Bollnow on "Die Citadelle Saint-Exupérys" and "Das Wohnen und Denken bei Heidegger", in: *Neue Geborgenheit*, pp. 164–168.

cendent as the firm ground on which he feels himself supported. In the middle of our action, space and time are transcended, and there are moments in which we experience the eternal. Naturally, the experience of the absolute in our manifold and versatile moods and activities does not mean that we comprehend it. We cannot constitute it as a subject or as subjective facticity, because we remain rooted in our changing experience. In all our reflections on ourselves and on the world, we have to start from our being-there and from the temporality and finiteness of our existence. In contradistinction to existential philosophy, however, Bollnow does not regard man as merely being thrown into the nothing. According to him, we are not merely thrown upon ourselves or related to ourselves and experience the transcendent through our very nothingness, as was believed to be the case in existential philosophy, but our being-there is now carried by the confidence we have in our fellowman and in the world surrounding us. Our existence is determined by our hope in the future and by our expectations, which stimulate us to creative action, which spur us to planning in time and encourage us to dwelling in space. In this ecstasy towards the transcendent, i.e., the standing out of the self towards the transcendent, we open ourselves to it. This means that we experience the transcendent through our experience of life, such as happiness, joy, contentment. These experiences transcend space and time. They are moments of self-fulfilment, in which we are linked with the absolute.

It may be said that Bollnow's philosophy of life is a philosohpy of balance. He agrees with Heidegger that the absolute cannot be constituted, but is experienced. But he disagrees with Heidegger in that he denies that it is experienced by anxiety and by care. He agrees that the human being-there is temporal, periodical and historical and that these adjectives form the authentic structure of human existence. He also concurs that human existence is one in anticipation of the future and that, for this matter, man is invariably directed towards the future. But he disagrees with Heidegger's thesis that this future (and thus man's existence) is determined by death or the nothing. Bollnow stresses the positive side of life and comes to the conclusion that anxiety and care are overruled by joy, happiness, confidence and hope, and that, through his positive experience, man regards the world as his home again, instead of feeling that he is thrown into the world as a stranger. The world is nothing hostile anymore, but, on the contrary, is that which carries him; and the future is no longer a menace or something that is dreaded, but it is precisely that which attracts man and which spurs him on to action. In striving for the future, man's esixtence, as one in anticipation of the future and, for this reason, one in antici- pation of himself, is changed from an existence-to-nothing in existential philosophy to an existence-to-being. Man's ability and courage to be, in the sense of living a full life and so coming to be himself, therefore, points beyond human experience. In regard to the problem of commu- nication, Bollnow is now able to point out that the feeling of anxiety, which Heidegger, in view of the acuteness of the crisis, makes man's fundamental experience, drives man back upon himself. Happiness and joy, on the other hand, open his mind to his fellowman and to the outside world. A smile for instance, will remove the separating walls between strangers.[29]

It is obvious that, in his attempt to overcome the acute experience of the crisis as it manifests itself in existential philosophy, Bollnow links up with Wilhelm Dilthey. Like the latter, Bollnow holds that metaphysics is dead. There is only a metaphysical consciousness or a metaphysical experience. The constitutive facticity of classical meta- physics may be said to have been replaced by an irrational facticity, taking its roots in human life. With Dilthey, this irrational facticity is the foundation of history. It is the cause of the constant widening of man's historical consciousness in the direction of the infinite(by the creation of ever new cultural systems). With Bollnow, this irrational facticity is the foundation of man's ontic experience. Dilthey's meta- physics of experience is of course also a reaction to the extreme position that was taken up by positivism. His method and field of investigation led to an autonomy of the humanities, which marked them off clearly from the natural sciences. Since Dilthey, *Verstehen* (understanding), *Erleben* (inner experience) and *Hermeneutik* (hermeneutics) are key words of the humanities and the humanistic method. Bollnow, too, makes use of the hermeneutic method in contradistinction to the ana- lytical method of the natural sciences and neo-positivist philosophy (logical positivism and naturalistic linguistics).[30] If neo-positivist philosophy dissolved the self into a linguistic analysis of man's beha-

---

[29] Although we based our remarks on Bollnow's philosophy mainly on *Neue Geborgenheit*, cf., especially in respect to the last observation, *Das Wesen der Stimmungen*. As to Bollnow's relation with existential philosophy, cf. *Existenzphilosopie*. A good exposition of Bollnow's philosophy is given in Patrick Kerans's doctoral dissertation: *La confiance selon Otto Friedrich Bollnow (Un essai de dépassement de l'existentialisme)*.

[30] With reference to hermeneutic logic, cf. Hans Lipps, *Untersuchungen zu einer hermeneu- tischen Logik*. Bollnow paid tribute to Lipps in an article entitled: "Die menschliche Natur, ein Beitrag zur philosophischen Lage der Gegenwart", in: *Blätter für deutsche Philosophie*, XVI (1942), pp. 293–312.

viour or man's various functions, Bollnow seeks to understand man's *Stimmungen* (moods) as an experience of the transcendent, which, as such, remains hidden. The authentic nature of man's existence, therefore, is rooted not in a negative experience of anxiety, as is the case in existential philosophy, nor is it described in terms of human behaviour, as is the case in the functionalist alternative, but it is understood in terms of man's inner experience. By emphasizing the positive experience of life, Bollnow seeks to free man from anxiety, and by stressing the importance in life of joy, happiness, confidence, hope, faith, composure, gratitude, the festive mood, etc., he attempts to restore his inner balance.

It must be admitted that Bollnow's alternative for dealing with the crisis, i.e., the restoration of our confidence in life, the world and the future, deserves our closest attention. It certainly is an effective way of dealing with a mankind that is ill in spirit and a world that has been hacked to pieces by the functionalistic method. Bollnow's anthropological approach of penetrating to the whole and, in this way, healing man and the world cannot be overlooked. But did he not overlook the controversial element in human activities? It is true that, by keeping an open mind for the existential root of human feeling and thinking, he showed the relativity of all human planning, acting and building. The house (culture) that man builds is always in danger of being destroyed again by the nothing. In Bollnow's philosophy, too, therefore, man had to be on the alert, but if man courageously took up the struggle against the nothing and made a clear decision in favour of life, the world and the future and had full confidence and faith in them, he was in no danger anymore of becoming the victim of anxiety, frustration and despair, but would be sound and healthy. It is then that he would experience a *neue Geborgenheit*, i.e., a new sense of security, which would have to be taken care of, however, lest it should be overwhelmed again by anxiety and frustration, which could easily wax strong again as a result of man's vulnerable position, i.e., as a result of the temporal and finite structure of his existence. Bollnow may be said to try to overcome the crisis by fusing man with the whole through his experience of the full life.[31]

But, we ask, does man's inner experience of life reflect the whole or does it, on the contrary, relativize the world and give it a subjective colouring? Is there a transcendent at all? How can we speak of it, if it is unknowable? Is this not as uncritical an assumption as is Heidegger's

---

[31] In this respect, cf. Bollnow's "Begriff des Heilen", in: *Neue Geborgenheit*, pp. 147–159.

assumption of an underlying absolute in his philosophy? It must also be pointed out here that Bollnow seems not to have appreciated sufficiently the importance of the absolute for human existence as *ek-sistence* in Heidegger's philosophy. For Heidegger's philosophy takes up a much more positive attitude towards life than it may appear to us at first sight. With Heidegger, too, it was not really the nothing that mattered in the end (the nothing was really only the result of the concealment of the absolute), but the whole into which man was embedded and to which he should keep himself open, thus rising above anxiety and frustation. But be that as it may, just as Heidegger constitutes human existence as the *ek-sistence* of being (in which one must in the final resort believe), Bollnow constitutes human life as the manifestation of being, in which one, too, must believe and have confidence. What Bollnow overlooks is the perspectivistic character of human truths. In what way man regards the world, life and human existence depends upon the method he applies. Does he, for instance, start from nature and describe natural events and their relations in terms of mathematics or linguistic propositions as do the sciences and functionalistic philosophy or does he start from man's being-there and work out man's existentials (the basic phenomena of human existence) from the negative side of human existence (its periodicity, temporality, historicity and perishability) as does existential philosophy or from the more positive side of human existence (the uplifting and transcendent nature of positive life experience) as does the philosophy of life? Man's view of the world, of life and of human existence also depends upon the situation in which man finds himself in a particular period. It depends upon the prevailing circumstances and the particular conflicts and problems in a particular epoch. If, for instance, man's material and rational needs have been oversaturated, man's irrational need reasserts itself, as is shown by the reaction of existential philosophy and the philosophy of life to the natural sciences and neo-positivist philosophy. Thus Bollnow's hermeneutic method, as a method of the humanities, stands in sharp contrast to the analytical method of the natural sciences and functionalistic philosophy.

If human truths as constitutions of the world in a particular existential situation are, however, always perspectivistic, it follows that they are always controversial. The bearing that this fact has on human knowledge and on human existence we shall investigate later on. For the time-being let it suffice to say that, if all constituted human truths are controversial, neither existential philosophy nor Bollnow's philosophy of life can possibly have overcome the crisis of truth. Both alternatives for dealing with the crisis are developed in a particular existential situation, i.e., under specific circumstances. Both philosophical alternatives ask specific questions in conformity with the specific problems they seek to solve or the particular conflicts they attempt to overcome. Both start from fixed premises and use definite methods upon which the outcome of their truth depends. These two philosophical alternatives are themselves related to one another, in as much as Bollnow's philosophy of life is a reaction to the existential alternative. Both alternatives stand thus in a controversial relation to one another. Hence, the crisis cannot have been overcome by any of these two alternatives for coping with it. If this is so, however, neither of them can possibly have guided man to live an authentic life; for each alternative sees the authentic nature of human existence in a different way, in accordance with its respective constituted world-view.

There is another prominent philosophical alternative for dealing with the crisis of truth which must be investigated, one that has come to be the accepted philosophy in half the world, namely, the Marxian alternative. We shall discuss this alternative under the heading: *Dialectical Alternative*. Let us see in what manner this philosophical approach grapples with the present crisis of truth and whether it may be said to have overcome it and thus to have solved the problem of the authenticity of human existence.

THE DIALECTICAL ALTERNATIVE

The dialectical alternative for dealing with the crisis of truth is historical by nature. In contradistinction to the functionalistic and existential alternatives, it is genetic and regards the historical process as the unfolding of an inherent historical logos or dialectical principle, the comprehension of which, on the part of man, leads to man's eventual liberation. In returning to its pure state, the logos gradually emancipates itself from its otherness, its externalization or its self-estrangement. The process of self-emancipation on the part of the logos simultaneously represents man's emancipation from his self-estrangement, since, by conceiving the logos as a rational principle, man blends with it and, so to speak, participates in this historical process.

With Hegel, this process is interpreted idealistically. According to Hegel, it is the absolute spirit that, as the absolute subject, objectivizes itself in history and in a dialectical movement, according to the principle: thesis-anithesis-synthesis, gives rise to the great historical epochs of culture, the Eastern, the Classical and the Christian epoch. Each epoch represents a higher degree of freedom. During the period of Eastern culture, it was only one that was really free (the despotic ruler); during the Classical age, it was a few that were free (the free citizens of the *polis* in contradistinction to the slaves); during the Christian period, however, all would be free, and this state of full freedom was regarded by Hegel as having been reached in Hegel's own time, the Romantic Christian era. In the period of Christian culture, the spirit had returned to itself and was completely free, pure and identical with itself. Accordingly, philosophy had fulfilled itself and, in the Christian era, was identical with religion. In the pure concept, which philosophy was now able to form of the absolute spirit, the universal truth of history had been realized and the *coincidentia oppositorum* (the synthesis of all antithetical concepts) was complete. This pure concept of the absolute, which man was capable of forming in his mind, reconciled the many with the one, the contingent with the necessary, the finite with the infinite, the immanent with the transcendent, knowledge with faith, philosophy with religion. In it, Truth, Reality, Beauty and Justice were combined.

Marx, as we have already seen, was dissatisfied with this projection of man into the clouds by Hegel. His contention was that the authentic nature of man's existence could not be derived from a universal concept, which was empty and had no concrete content. The authenticity of human existence could not be constituted theoretically. Man would be free and would be able to live an authentic life only if he was in step with the practice, i.e., the real needs of the people, as they were felt at the time. Marx criticizes Hegel's idealistic dialectic as follows: "Diese Bewegung (of the historical spirit) in ihrer abstrakten Form als Dialektik gilt daher als das *wahrhaft menschliche Leben*, und weil es doch eine Abstraktion, eine Entfremdung des menschlichen Lebens ist, gilt es als *göttlicher Prozess*, daher als der göttliche Prozess des Menschen.... Dieser Prozess muss einen Träger haben, ein Subjekt ....das sich als absolutes Selbstbewusstsein wissende Subjekt ist daher der *Gott, absoluter Geist, die sich wissende betätigende Idee*. Der wirkliche Mensch und die wirkliche Natur werden bloss zu Prädikaten, zu Symbolen dieses verborgnen unwirklichen Menschen und dieser unwirklichen Natur."[1]

As man's needs were at the time of a predominantly material nature, it is not surprising that Karl Marx, together with Friedrich Engels, interpreted the historical process in a materialist way. Marx contended that Hegel's idealist dialectic suited only the few that were in possession of the means of production, the capitalists, who were interested in the *status quo*. Hegel's dialectic thus formed the ideological superstructure of bourgeois society or the ideology of the possessing class. This ideological superstructure helped them to retain their privileged social position, to uphold their private interest and to retain political power. This superstructure of the ruling class was in sharp conflict and contradiction with the infrastructure of the productive class, the *proletariat*. This latter class was estranged from itself, in as much as it had no control over the means of production and could not dispose of its own products. Its members were not human beings but a commodity. In order to "subsist" they sold their labour in the open market in competition

---

1 "Kritik der Hegelschen Dialektik und Philosophie überhaupt", in: *Karl Marx, Ausgewählte Schriften*, p. 201.

with their colleagues, sometimes at an appallingly low price. Their products did not belong to them, but to the owner of the factory or the means of production. He sold them at a profit by exploiting the workers as much as possible. The latter had to purchase their own products at yet a higher price from the trader, who also wanted to make a profit. It can thus be seen that the crisis consisted in the unbridgeable gulf between the private individual interests of the owners of the means of production, the financiers and the traders, i.e., the middle class in general on the one hand, and the collective universal interests of the working class on the other. Only if the private ownership of the means of production and private property as such were abolished and the means of production were in the hands of the working class and were used in the collective, universal interests instead of in the private, individual interests of a few, would the social rupture be healed. Only then would the proletariat (which in an industrial society formed the vast majority of the population) be free to determine its own destiny. Only if this happened, would the workers be fully-fledged men and would they be able to lead an authentic existence. And only if the goods of production belonged to those who produced them, could there be a just distribution of these goods and could the needs of all be catered for, so that people were freed from want, suffering and pain. If the means of production were controlled by the producers, the length of working hours could be reduced, and all men, not only the idle rich, would have time for the pursuit of cultural interests and for recreation. In this way, they would be able to gratify their intellectual, aesthetical and spiritual needs as well.[2]

From this it becomes clear what Marx and Engels meant by materialism. It could be defined as *the self-creation of man as a productive being*. In Marx's and Engel's dialectical materialism, the historical logos manifests itself in man's gradual advancement through labour from the slave, the serf, the middle class burgher to the communist labourer. As the latter, man has attained absolute freedom and, as fully fledged man, leads an authentic existence. That is to say, by the gradual improvement of the means of production, which determine the way of production, the structure of society changes. When the process of improvement of the means of production has reached a certain climax, this quantitative process of evolution suddenly changes into revolution, whereby the old ruling class is overthrown and its place is taken by

---

[2] With reference to the estrangement of man on account of private ownership, cf. K. Marx, "Zur Kritik der Nationalökonomie", in: *Karl Marx, Ausgewählte Schriften*, pp. 110–180.

the new productive class. Thus, sudden change of the evolutionary process into revolution represents a change from quantity to quality. For by it, the old social structure is superseded by a new one. This sudden change of evolution into revolution on the grounds of the changed means of production is conceived as a necessary motion of history, according to the dialectical principle: Thesis, anithesis, synthesis. It is in this way that the feudal society was born in the lap of the slaveholder society and that the bourgeois society sprang from the womb of the feudal society. Due to growing industrialization, the increasing automation of the means of production and the capitalist way of production, bourgeois society has given birth to a new social class, the proletariat. The latter class forms the basis of the new communist society, which will inevitably develop within a bourgeois society as the negation of the negation, i.e., as overcoming the conflicts and contradictions that inevitably exist within a bourgeois society.[3]

It is thus obvious that the proletariat is the new historical force which, according to Marx and Engels, brings about the transition from capitalism to communism. In order to carry out its historical mission, the proletariat must at first become class-conscious, which it is not immediately. It must at first learn to distinguish between its *immediate* interests (the immediate improvement of its economic situation within the capitalist system) and its *real* interests (to free itself from capitalist rule by gaining control over the means of production itself). Herbert Marcuse writes on this point: "The Marxian distinction between real and immediate interest is of the greatest importance for understanding the relationship between theory and practice, between strategy and tactics in Marxism. The distinction implies a historical conflict between theory and practice, the origin and solution of which lie in the development of capitalism....... If the societal relationships determine consciousness, they do so also with respect to the proletariat. And if the societal relationships are class relationships, they also introduce the discrepancy between the form in which reality *appears* to men and the 'essence' of reality. The discrepancy between essence and phenomena is the cornerstone of the Marxian method, but the metaphysical categories have become sociological ones..... As applied to the proletariat, although it is 'in reality' the negation of the capitalist system, this objective reality will not immediately appear in the proletarian

---

[3] In regard to the necessary relation between productive forces and social conditions, cf. K. Marx, "Das Elend der Philosophy", in: K. Marx/F. Engels, *Werke*, vol.4 Berlin 1959, p. 138

consciousness – the 'class in itself' is not necessarily 'class for itself.'"[4]

Marcuse points out further that Marx and Engels were fully aware of the gulf between phenomena and essence, or else theory and practice, as the majority of the proletariat was still immature (imbued with capitalist ideas). But both thinkers believed that the class-consciousness of the proletariat would be gradually awakened as contradictions and conflicts within the capitalist system became more severe. The proletariat would then constitute itself as a revolutionary class, and, by means of direct organized action, would establish a socialist society.[5] By fulfilling its historical mission, humanity (the proletariat) has (according to Marx's and Engels's philosophy) bridged the gulf between its immediate and its real interest, between phenomena and essence, between theory and practice. Universal truth has been realized, so man is no longer estranged from the world, from society and from himself. In accordance with the principle of identity, man has realized himself to the full and leads an authentic existence.

Marx and Engels make the assertion that their historical materialism represents an objective view of the historical process. They teach that the class-struggle and the class structure within human society, which manifest themselves in the economics, the politics and the ruling ideology of a particular social system, are not something that is read into the socio-historical process, but are its inner objective law. The socio-historical dialectical motion, which is the result of changing economic conditions (which in turn determine the superstructure, i.e., the political outlook and ideology of the ruling class) corresponds to the inner motion of matter, which is registered by the sciences in the form of dialectical laws. The homogeneity of Marxian dialectical materialism may be stated as follows: The development of the sciences as the growing exploration of objective natural laws determine the economic and social conditions as objective historical laws. The sciences are thus conceived as having a historical aspect, while history is regarded as being scientific.

That Marx and Engels conceived the historical process in terms of objective laws, which process by necessity leads to a final stage, transpires from the following: "Marx und Engels erklärten die Existenz und

---

[4] *Soviet Marxism*, pp. 23–24.

[5] Not necessarily by violence, as it appears from a number of pronouncements by Marx and Engels, e.g., Marx's speech at Amsterdam (1872); "Konspekt der Debatten über das Sozialistengesetz" (1878); Engels "Introduction to Marx's Class Struggles in France" and "Critique of the Social Democratic Draft Program," 1891, Sect. II.

den Ursprung der Klassen, aber auch den historisch vorübergehenden Charakter der Klassenstruktur der Gesellschaft wissenschaftlich. Sie bewiesen, dass der Klassenkampf eine objective Gesetzmässigkeit der Entwicklung jeder Gesellschaft darstellt, deren ökonomische Grundlage das Privateigentum an Produktionsmitteln ist... Das Hauptsächlichste im Marxismus ist die Lehre, dass der Klassenkampf notwendig zur Diktatur des Proletariats führt, dass diese Diktatur den Übergang zur Aufhebung aller Klassen, zu einer Gesellschaft ohne Klassen darstellt.''[6] The question now arises whether the objective historical necessity discovered by Marx and Engels is really objective in the sense of existing independently of man's consciousness and reason and is reflected in man's consciousness or, as Marx and Engels would say: whether being (social conditions) determine man's consciousness? There is of course no doubt that our thinking is influenced by our environment, but when it comes to the constitution of laws in the sciences and in history, it cannot be denied that their "universal" character depends upon the premise from which we constitute these laws and upon the method which we thereby apply. The Marxian premise from which the dialectical principle of history is constituted is the economic one. That is to say that, in Marxism, man is regarded as essentially a productive being, who, by his productive activity, determines the whole structure of history and of society, and the method that is to be applied in order to comprehend the socio-historical process as a universal truth is the dialectical one.

We cannot help establishing that Marx overcomes the crisis of truth by the constitution of history as a necessary dialectical process and, in this sense, as a universal truth. The dialectical motion of history is fully comprehended by him, and this comprehension enables him to anticipate the course and purpose of history. In other words, Marx "knows" the course and purpose of history *because* he has constituted it himself as a dialectical principle. By grasping it as such, Marx disposes of it and subsumes it under the *law of identity*. Eberhard Grisebach has unmasked the true character of the dialectical method when he says about the dialectical principle: "Es handelt sich um ein absolutes Prinzip, denn der absolute Anspruch auf Herrschaft und Verständnis des Daseins ist mit dieser Erkenntnisvoraussetzung gemacht. Es handelt sich wieder um eine metaphysische Erkenntnis, die ihre Grenzen überschreitet, und zwar nur deshalb, weil man die wirkliche Notlage der Gegenwart durch die Voraussetzung der Spannung vermeiden wollte. Der Versuch ist zwar geglückt, die ehemaligen Herrschaftsansprüche

---

[6] *Geschichte der Philosopie*, ed. by the Academy of U. S. S. R., vol. III, p. 236.

durchzusetzen und zu retten, aber es geschah auf Kosten der Wirk-lichkeit."[7] In accordance with this critical appreciation of the dialec-tical method by Grisebach, it is permissible to say that Marx has over-come the crisis of truth no less in his imagination than has Hegel. What he has done is that he has inverted Hegel's method by giving it a mate-rialist basis. It makes, however, no difference whether the historical logos is constituted from an idealistic or a materialist premise. Both constitutions are absolute and dogmatic. As methodological projections of the human consciousness and the human self in a particular existen-tial situation, they are both relative truths, in as much as they reflect the specific conflicts and problems of the age in which they were con-ceived. They are both philosophical alternatives for coping with these specific conflicts and problems. As such, they are controversial, which has already been shown by the fact that Marx's perspective, in its own turn, provoked new contradiction and gave rise to the projection of new perspectives.

Is it then not the controversial relation that holds among the various truth-perspectives that points to reality rather than the artifical over-coming of the crisis of truth by the dialectical method? But this ques-tion will occupy as at a later stage. For the time being let us establish the fact that Marx's dialectical alternative for coping with the specific crisis of his time (that of the conflict between the bourgeois class and the working class) has not settled the crisis of truth and has therefore failed to resolve the crisis of man. On the contrary, it has given rise to fresh controversy and has created new problems for man to solve. Moreover, the actual course history has taken seems not to have borne out Marx's dialectical law as he constituted it, as we shall see presently.

Whether or not the course history has taken is exactly as Marx had constituted and in this way forecast it, can be tested in the light of the question whether capitalist society has actually changed into socialist society, thereby by necessity superseding it, or whether the capitalist system has not even gained in strentgh and has consolidated its posi-tion. – Already Marx had taught that capitalism develops "counter-trends" against its inherent contradictions. Such countertrends are, for example, capital export, monopolies, government intervention.[8] In addition, one factor in capitalist society had been overlooked and gross-ly neglected, namely, the large peasant class. It was these two factors

---

[7] *Gegenwart*, pp. 153–154.

[8] In this connection, cf. Karl Marx, *Das Kapital*, Buch III, especially the chapters "Ge-setz des tendenziellen Falls der Profitrate als solches" and "Die Rolle des Kredits in der kapi-talistischen Produktion."

that played an important part in determining the future structure of both capitalism and socialism and in influencing the way in which the controversy between the two systems was carried on.

The countertrends of capitalism, which, according to Marx, would result in the growing exploitation and impoverishment of the proletariat and, for this reason, would accelerate its impending crisis and bring about its eventual downfall, had turned out to be stabilizing factors. Contrary to Marx's expectations, the countertrends of capitalism had strengthened the capitalist system to such an extent that it was conceived by Marxian theorists as having entered a new stage. It was said to have moved from capitalism to *imperialism*. "The main features of the (new) stage," writes Marcuse, "were said to be the transformation of free into regimented competition, dominated by national and international cartels, trusts, and monopolies, the amalgamation between banking and industrial capital, government and business, and an expansionist economic policy toward 'noncapitalist' and weaker capitalist areas (e.g., intensified exploitation of colonial and dependent countries.")[9] Marxian theory had to readjust itself to these developments. There were two alternatives for dealing with the new situation, which caused a split within Marxian ranks. The reformists, led by Eduard Bernstein, held that the proletariat could improve its economic and political position within the framework of the organized (political) capitalist system itself and would be able to establish a socialist society by constitutional means. It was hoped that it would be able to do so by the increasing economic and political influence of organized labour.[10] The orthodox Marxians, on the other hand, came to the conclusion that any compromise with the capitalist class could only benefit the latter and was treason to the working class. This wing was led by Vladimir Iljitsch Lenin, the founder of Soviet Marxism. Marcuse says "The emergence of Leninism as a new form of Marxism is determined by two main factors: (1) the attempt to draw the peasantry into the orbit of Marxian theory and strategy, and (2) the attempt to redefine the prospects of capitalist and revolutionary development in the imperialist era."[11]

While Marx had predicted the growing revolutionary potential of the working class on account of its increasing impoverishment and exploi-

[9] *Soviet Marxism*, p. 28.
[10] Cf. Eduard Bernstein, *Evolutionary Socialism: A Criticism and Affirmation*. Bernstein's theory of economic democracy was expounded by Rudolf Hilferding at the Kiel Conference of the German Social Democratic Party in 1927.
[11] *Soviet Marxism*, p. 29.

tation by the capitalist class,[12] the opposite process had taken place. It was because of the receding revolutionary potential of the working class as a result of the growing prosperity in the highly industrialized countries of the West that Lenin shifted the revolutionary accent to the backward countries. In accordance with conditions in Russia, where the industrial proletariat was greatly outnumbered by the peasants, many of whom were semi-serfs, he proclaimed the worker-peasant alliance. In the face of the receding revolutionary potential of the working class in the highly industrialized countries of the West, Lenin came to the conclusion that the revolution stood the best chance in a backward country like Russia, where there was the greatest resentment against the ruling classes. But in the face of the strengthened position of capitalism, Lenin argued that the class-consciousness of the proletariat would not be aroused from within, as Marx had taught, but must be brought to the proletariat from without. The proletariat must be led in its historical mission by a revolutionary *avantgarde*, the communist party, which would lay down the revolutionary strategy and tactics that were to be followed in the struggle against capitalism and imperialism.[13] Lenin believed that imperialistic capitalism would eventually destroy itself through its inherent contradictions, which sprang from selfish interests. After having accomplished the revolution in one country, the revolutionary communist party must thus adopt the right strategy and apply the proper tactics in view of the "objective" crisis situation in the capitalist world, with a view to overthrowing the capitalist system altogether.

In view of the above, Lenin's uncomprising attitude against "economism" and "collaborationism" of the "reformists" and "revisionists," e.g., Rudolf Hilferding and Karl Kautzky, becomes understandable. His theories on the strategy and tactics of the revolution in the face of imperialism laid the foundation for socialism in one country, which was expounded most forcefully by Stalin later on. In order to develop the class consciousness of the worker and to entrench firmly Soviet rule as the rule of the proletariat, which had been estab-

[12] In this regard, cf. *Manifest der Kommunistischen Partei,* esp. par. I, "Bourgeois und Proletarier" and par. II "Proletarier und Kommunisten". In the *Communist Manifesto,* the dialectical relationship between capital and wage labour, bourgeoisie and proletariat and the historical necessity of the proletarian revolution are succinctly stated, and it is shown that "Mit der Entwicklung der grossen Industrie wird also unter den Füssen der Bourgeoisie die Grundlage selbst weggezogen, worauf sie produziert und die Produkte sich aneignet. Sie produziert vor allem ihre eigenen Totengräber. Ihr Untergang und der Sieg des Proletariats sind gleich unvermeidlich".

[13] Lenin propounded these ideas in "Was tun?", in: W. J. Lenin, *Werke,* vol. 5, p. 436

lished by the October Revolution in 1917, a stepping up of the process of industrialization in Russia was necessary. Hence Lenin's definition of socialism as "electrification plus Soviet power."

Lenin saw in the October Revolution the beginning of the world revolution and believed that he could establish socialism firmly in Russia only if the West, too, turned socialist. Stalin, Lenin's successor, no longer believed in a socialist revolution in the West. He, therefore, advocated the doctrine of socialism in one country, which he hoped to achieve by the stamping out of the independent, property-owning peasants (the Kulaks) and by bureaucratization, industrialization and compulsory collectivization of farms. Thereby the classical Marxian theory was totally perverted and converted into its opposite. The idea of the spontaneity, objectivity and inner necessity of socio-historical processes was replaced by the "cult of the leader," by arbitrariness and by the dictatorship of one person: "Die Elektrifizierung verschlang die Sowjets. . . Der Stalinismus proklamierte das Primat des Politischen über das Ökonomische, des Willens über die Wirklichkeit. Das Bewusstsein, der sozialistische Wille der Führung, wurde von aussen in die Wirklichkeit getragen, um sie im Sinne totalitärer Gestaltung zu ändern."[14]

The thesis of socialism in one country can be regarded as an admission of the failure of the Marxian theory in respect of actual historical developments. In fact, the failure of the Marxian theory already became manifest in Lenin's doctrine itself, not only from the necessity which he found in having to readjust Marxism to a situation which had not been anticipated by Marx, but also from the inherent contradictions in Lenin's actual doctrine. In this respect, Marcuse points out that the development of Soviet Marxism was decided by the fact that the revolutionary potential of the industrial working class receded throughout the advanced capitalist world on account of the growing prosperity in the capitalist countries. He observes that Lenin underestimated the economic and political potentialities of capitalism and the change in the position of the proletariat and so failed to draw the theoretical conclusion from the changed situation. Lenin's attempt to save the classical notion of Marxism caused a gap between theory and practice in Soviet Marxism. "For, while Lenin from the beginning of his activity reoriented the revolutionary strategy of his party in accordance with the new situation, his theoretical conception did not follow suit. Lenin's retention of the classical notion of the revolutionary proletariat, sus-

[14] B. Goldenberg, *Karl Marx Ausgewählte Schriften*, Einleitung, pp. 54–55.

tained with the help of the theory of the labor aristocracy and the avant garde, revealed its inadequacy from the beginning. Even prior to the First World War it became clear that the 'collaborationist' part of the proletariat was quantitatively and qualitatively different from a small upper stratum that had been corrupted by monopoly capital, and that the Social Democratic Party and trade union bureaucracy were more than 'traitors' – rather that their policy reflected pretty exactly the economic and social condition of the majority of the organized working classes in the advanced industrial countries."[15]

This makes it clear that Marx's constitution of the historical process was not endorsed by the actual historical situation and that, in this way, the objective character of Marxian dialectic was called in question. In fact, the question arises whether the capitalist system is doomed to self-destruction by historical necessity. Lenin tried to save the objective character of the Marxian doctrine by clinging to this historical necessity. But did not the very necessity of having had to readjust Marx's teaching to a situation not anticipated by Marx and so having had to recast it in a somewhat different mould point to the constitutive and therefore subjective nature of Marx's doctrine? In trying to keep in step with modern developments in the natural sciences, Lenin, apart from having to reformulate Marx's economic, social and revolutionary doctrines, also had to show that these developments were in line with dialectical materialism. This attempt had to be made if the scientific character of dialectical materialism was to be maintained. This enterprise on the part of Lenin shed a broad light on the controversy of truth that was going on in Lenin's time. It laid bare the controversial relationship in which Soviet Marxism stands with the functionalistic alternative for coping with the crisis of truth, namely, positivism and neo-positivism.

The attempt to show how modern science corroborated and endorsed the teachings of dialectical materialism was made by Lenin in his chief philosophical work *Materialism and Empiriocriticism*. Already Friedrich Engels, in his work *Herrn Eugen Dührings Umwälzungen der Wissenschaft*, generally known as *Anti-Dühring*, defined dialectic as the science of the general laws of motion and development in nature, in history (society) and in human thinking.[16] Lenin, in *Materialism and Empiriocritisism*, seeks to show that scientific laws are the reflec-

---

[15] Marcuse, *Soviet Marxism*, pp. 30–31.

[16] P. 25 f. –In this work, Engels posits the dialectical categories of thinking against the fixed "metaphysical" categories of positivist thinking. He polemicizes that dialectical logic is a necessary presupposition for objective, scientific thinking.

tion in our minds of the objective motion of matter, of its quantitative changes that result in different qualitative structures or properties. From this premise, Lenin attempts to show that only dialectical materialism draws the correct philosophical conclusions from the modern developments in the natural sciences and that "empiriocriticism" (positivism and neo-Kantianism) fails to do so on account of its idealistic and subjective starting-point.

Through its motion, matter assumes various properties, such as mass, energy, life, consciousness. By scientific experimentation, man penetrates deeper and deeper into the intrinsic motions of matter and becomes more and more conscious of them. Hence, there is nothing that, on principle, is beyond the reach of human knowledge. There is no transcendent, and, therefore, no metaphysics. There is no God, but man depends entirely upon himself. It may be said that, in Marxism-Leninism, faith in God has been replaced by faith in scientific progress. Because the world is reflected in man's mind, man is able to change the world, and, in so doing, changes himself. There exists between man and the world a dialectical relationship, which is experienced as a creative tension. Conditions in the world determine man's consciousness, and man's consciousness in turn fashions the world. Scientific research and activity in Marxism-Leninism mean to bring about the eventual identity of man and the world in such a way that man is in full control of it. By changing the world into a scientific world, the sciences and technology change man into a scientific and technological being, whose interests coincide with those of modern scientific and technological society. In Marxism-Leninism, therefore, the sciences have not merely epistemological meaning, but also economic, political and sociological significance. There is in the conception of Soviet science a distinct pragmatic note. As in classical Marxism, truth in Soviet Marxism has a universal character. Man gains functional control over nature by gradually getting to know its laws of motion and change through science. Being in full comprehension of the natural laws, man is free from oppression, want and suffering. He is in harmony with nature and society and is so leading an authentic existence.

It may well be argued that Soviet truth, like positivist truth, is also functionalistic by nature, in as much, as it, too, aims at bringing nature under man's functional control. But unlike the truth of the functionalist alternative for coping with the crisis of truth, it does not claim to be neutral, but, on the contrary, insists upon its being partial. It does not merely describe natural events in piecemeal fashion or trace the functional relations of the propositions describing these events, as is the case in positivist philosophy, but it constitutes the dialectical law of progress and passionately takes its side. Unlike positivist philosophy, it does not seek to overcome the crisis of truth by conforming to the *status quo*, but it endeavours to end the crisis by overcoming the *status quo*. It believes that, by overcoming the *status quo* (the capitalist system with its inherent conflicts) and by the acquisition of absolute knowledge of the world, truth is realized and a just society will be established, in which all human needs are met. The *principle of partiality*, which Lenin posited against the "dishonest neutrality and impartiality" of "bourgeois" (positivist) philosophy, meant that Marxian philosophy must keep in step with the progressive forces and take their side, for only in so doing can it reflect objective reality.[17] It must fight the forces of obscurantism and idealism of bourgeois philosophy (which today are embodied in existential philosophy and neo-positivism), and it must be firmly on the side of the proletariat, which is the only progressive class and the interests of which coincide with the interests of the whole. "Diesem Prinzip (of partiality) folgend, verbinden die marxistischen Philosophen die Ausarbeitung des dialektischen Materialismus eng mit dem Kampf gegen die bürgerliche Philosophie und gegen revisionistische und dogmatische Verzerrungen. Sie entlarven die unaufrichtige, gleisnerische 'Neutralität' und 'Unparteilichkeit', mit der die Feinde des historischen Fortschritts das reaktionäre Klassenwesen ihrer philosophischen Ansichten zu verschleiern und zu maskieren suchen."[18]

The central point of Lenin's polemic against the positivists and neo-Kantians in M*aterialism and Empiriocriticism* seems to be his endeavour to expose the partiality of these thinkers as fellow-travellers or even active supporters of bourgeois society and the capitalist system. In reference to Berkeley and also to Hume, Lenin tries to prove that the more modern positivists and neo-Kantians, e.g., Friedrich Lange, Richard Avenarius, Ernst Mach, Henri Poincaré, are in reality subjective idealists. He argues that their philosophy lends itself to maintaining the *status quo* and, for this matter, to keeping in power the reactionary forces in society. In reference to the scientific discoveries of his time, Lenin seeks to demonstrate that only dialectical materialism

---

[17] In this connection, cf. *Materialismus und Empiriokritizismus*, especially "Parteien in der Philosophie und philosophische Wirrköpfe", pp. 339-350.
[18] *Geschichte der Philosophie*, ed. by the Academy of the Sciences of the U. S. S. R., vol. VI, p. 146.

can draw the right conclusions from the latest developments in the sciences, and, for this reason, is the only true scientific philosophy. In caustic language, he criticizes Mach's and Avenarius's premise, namely, that our sensations and the relations that hold between them are the only source of knowledge and that knowledge means tracing the functional relations in our sense-experience. Lenin points out that this starting-point is not new at all, but is identical with Berkeley's *esse est percipi* and with Hume's sensationalism and agnosticism. Lenin also criticizes Poincaré, who regards scientific laws as mere conventions and symbols, which have value in as far as they function successfully. Lenin regards all these starting-points as idealistic, in as much as their advocates see in man's consciousness the only source of knowledge and, consequently, deny the existence of matter outside sense-experience, or refuse to commit themselves on that point (agnosticism).

This subjective approach is regarded as dangerous by Lenin, in as much as it deprives man of the objective source of knowledge, namely, matter, as it is reflected in man's consciousness in its motion, and, for this reason, clears the way for dogmatism, obscurantism and fideism. It bars the road to progress and to true knowledge. It supports the *status quo.* "Der Unterschied zwischen Materialismus und 'Machismus,'" says Lenin, "besteht also in dieser Frage (whether, in regard to knowledge, matter or the senses are the primary source) in folgendem. Der Materialismus betrachtet in vollem Einklang mit der Naturwissenschaft als das ursprünglich Gegebene die Materie, als das Sekundäre – Bewusstsein, Denken, Empfindung; denn die Empfindung ist in klar ausgeprägter Form nur mit den höchsten Formen der Materie (der organischen Materie) verbunden, und in den 'Grundsteinen des Gebäudes der Materie' kann man nur die Existenz einer Fähigkeit, die der Empfindung ähnlich ist, annehmen."[19] In this connection, Lenin refers to the monistic world-view of the biologists Ernst Häckel and Lloyd Morgan.

In Lenin's polemic against the positivists and the neo-Kantians, the decisive difference between the functionalistic alternative and the dialectical alternative in regard to the problem of truth and knowledge becomes clear. Both approaches purport to be anti-metaphysical. Both recognize only one world and not a double world of immanent truth on the one hand and the transcendent on the other. Both alternatives base their theories on the natural sciences. The positivists, however, from Mach, Avenarius, Kirchhoff right up to the contemporary

[19] Lenin, *Materialismus und Empiriokritizismus*, p. 37.

logical positivists and naturalistic linguists, strive to achieve their aim of gaining objective knowledge by the most economical description of man's sense-experience or of man's language and, in this sense, make use of William Occam's famous razor. The dialectical materialists, on the other hand, try to reach this aim by getting to know the objective laws of the motion of nature (matter), as they are reflected in man's consciousness. The dialectical interplay between changing nature and changing consciousness will eventually result in their convergence. Whereas the dialectical materialists accuse the empiricists of subjectivism and idealism, which means that they are unscientific, the neopositivists reply that the idea of a self-propelling matter is a metaphysical concept and an unverifiable assumption. Lenin categorically rejects the claim of the positivists to neutrality and objectivity and ridicules their belief that, by the concept of experience, they have overcome the contradiction between idealism and materialism "Zu bedauern sind nur die Leute, die Avenarius und Co. geglaubt haben, dass man durch das Wort 'Erfahrung' die 'veraltete' Unterscheidung von Materialismus und Idealismus überwinden könne" or even more clearly "Das Wort 'Erfahrung,' auf dem die Machisten ihre Systeme aufbauen, diente schon seit langem zur Verhüllung der idealistischen Systeme und dient jetzt bei Avenarius und Co. dazu, den eklektischen Übergang vom idealistischen Standpunkt zum Materialismus zu ermöglichen und umgekehrt. Die verschiedenen 'Definitionen' dieses Begriffs drücken nur die beiden Grundlinien in der Philosophie aus (idealism and materialism), die Engels so glänzend aufgedeckt hat."[20]

In the paragraph entitled "Die Krise der modernen Physik,"[21] Lenin traces this crisis to the disappearance of matter as a result of the idealist starting-point of the empiricists. All the problems that arise in physics in regard to principles such as Lavoisier's principle of the conservation of mass, which was said to have been undermined by the electronic theory of matter, would not emerge if objective reality as existing outside the mind had not been given up. According to Lenin, the crisis in modern physics is to be ascribed to the vanishing of matter. According to contemporary dialectical materialism, this observation holds true also for the problems of contemporary physics, e.g., the wave-particle problem and the problem of causality, which is closely related to it. If, for example, the two aspects of wave and particle, as they appear in the electron or the photon, are merely confronted with

20 *Materialismus und Empiriokritizismus*, pp. 144–146.
21 *Op. cit.*, pp. 251–257.

one another in terms of mathematical description and thus become two fixed costructions of our minds, which logically exclude one another, it is not surprising that all kinds of puzzles arise, e.g., the difficulty of coinciding place and time in electronic events, which finds expression in Heisenberg's relation of uncertainty, and which has shaken the classical concept of causality. In order to get out of the dilemma of the wave-particle dualism, Max Born, for instance, holds that wave and particle are complementary to one another.[22] Dialectical materialism holds, however, that the phenomena of wave and particle are two different states in the motion of the electron and that, if electronic events were regarded in an objective genetic way, no such puzzles and problems would arise.

Dialectical materialism thus holds that the crisis in modern physics must be traced to the abstraction of our experience from its objective source by mathematical or logical (functional) description. This mechanical piecemeal description of natural phenomena in the case of the electron, for instance, leads to the confrontation in a static manner of two aspects of one and the same natural event, which are in reality only two different states (properties) of one and the same dynamic matter. If matter were seen as genetic and objective in the sense of changing from one qualitative state into another, instead of being viewed subjectively in terms of our conscious experiences, the truth-functions of which are established by mathematical description, there would be no unsurmountable barriers between the two phenomena of wave and particle. One phenomena would no longer logically exclude the other one. If we become aware that the dynamic motion of matter is reflected in our mind in the form of dialectical laws, which science is able to explore, problems such as the subject-object problem, determinism and indeterminism, the thing-in-itself, matter, mass and energy, the problems of absoluteness and relativity, infinity and finiteness, continuity and discontinuity, would no longer baffle scientists and philosophers. The world is one; nature and man, science and history are referred to one another by the dialectical motion of matter.[23]

---

[22] Cf. *Von der Verantwortung des Naturwissenschaftlers*, pp. 101–108.

[23] Already Lenin wrote: "Doch der dialektische Materialismus betont nachdrücklich, dass jede wissenschaftliche These über die Struktur und die Eigenschaften der Materie nur annähernde, relative Geltung hat, dass es in der Natur keine absoluten Schranken gibt, dass die sich bewegende Materie Verwandlungen durchmacht aus einem Zustand in einen anderen, der von unserem Standpunkt aus scheinbar mit dem vorangegangenen unvereinbar ist u.s.w.... Die neue Physik ist hauptsächlich gerade deshalb zum Idealismus abgeglitten, weil die Physiker die Dialektik nicht kannten..... Indem sie die Unveränderlichkeit der bis dahin bekannten Elemente und Eigenschaften der Materie verneinten, gelangten sie zur Verneinung der Materie, das heisst der objektiven Realität der physischen Welt. Indem sie den absoluten

All in all, it becomes clear that Leninism and Soviet Marxism in general ascribe the existence of unsolvable problems in contemporary science to a wrong approach. The strict empirical functionalism, which we encounter, for instance, in Russel's *monistic neutralism*, where the distinction between mind and matter becomes blurred, is to the dialectical materialists a disguised idealism. The descriptive method dissolves everything into functional relations and, for this reason, cannot recognize matter as existing outside human experience or human consciousness. If, however, an objective self-propelling matter were recognized as being reflected in the human consciousness and hence as the source of our knowledge, there would be no unsolvable problems any longer. But to the positivist philosophers, the conception of a self-propelling matter is a metaphysical construction, which transcends our experience, in terms of which alone "facts" can be related to each other by either mathematical or linguistic propositions.

In discussing the functionalistic alternative for coping with the crisis of truth, we have already shown that, in positivist thinking, truth is no less constructed from a fixed underlying premise than is the case in any philosophical approach or alternative, and this applies to the dialectical approach as well. It, too, in its own terms, is actually idealistic. By that is meant that, like any other philosophical perspective, it really starts from consciousness when ordering the world in a rational manner and constituting it as an immanent truth in a particular existential situation. Dialectical materialism can make the optimistic assertion that man is capable of absolute knowledge of the world and so able to gain absolute control over it only because the dialectical materialists have themselves worked out in their minds the structure of the world and the dialectical pattern of history. It is true that this rational constitution of the world and of history "solves" problems such as the structure of matter, the problem of life and of human consciousness. But this solution is one only in theory, not in practice. It is found by the very constitution of the world on a particular premise and by a specific method. In the case of dialectical materialism, it is by reducing the events of nature and of history to the basic event of self-propelling matter that the phenomena of life and of human con-

Character der wichtigsten und fundamentalen Gesetze verneinten, gerieten sie dahin, jede Gesetzmässigkeit in der Natur zu verneinen, die Naturgesetze für blosse Konvention...... auszugeben. Indem sie auf dem annähernden, relativen Charakter unseres Wissens bestanden, gelangten sie zur Verneinung des von der Erkenntnis unabhängigen Objekts, das von dieser Erkenntnis annähernd getreu, relativ richtig widergespiegelt wird. Usw. usf. ohne Ende". (*Materialismus und Empiriokritizismus*, pp. 261–262).

sciousness can be explained as properties of matter in a specific state of motion. The phenomena of life and consciousness are thus only definite qualitative changes of matter which took place during its process of evolution; and it is on that account that dialectical materialism can declare the human mind to be the highest developed matter. But in order to conceive life and the mind as properties of matter in a specific state of its motion, it is necessary that we adopt the Marxian premise of an *objective* matter in motion that exists independently of us. It is, however, exactly this premise which cannot be proved.

If, however, the dialectical alternative for coping with the crisis of truth can be shown to construct truth from an assumed premise, it cannot claim, as indeed it does, that it has resolved the crisis; at least it has not done so in reality, but only in theory. The total character, however, of this theory even sharpens the crisis. This total character is due to the metaphysical nature of dialectical materialism, no matter how much this is denied by the dialectical materialists. The metaphysical nature of dialectical materialism is shown by the identification of being and thinking, i.e., that, by the comprehension of the dialectical principle as the constitutive factor of the world and of history, man is blended with the world and with history, or else that the rational nature of the world and of history are reflected in his mind. At this last stage, when all problems are solved and all conflicts and contradictions have been overcome, man is absolutely free and happy. At this stage, he has been changed from a selfish, egocentric being into a social being with a social consciousness, whose interests coincide with the general interest. The question arises, however, whether such a change of consciousness, in which the individual interest is identical with the social interest, is humanly possible. Is it not only a beautiful dream, which, instead of leading man to an authentic existence, results in new unauthenticity, self-estrangement and deception? Are not the self-assertion of the individual and the pursuit of private interests the very criteria of man's humanity? Can human beings still be called men in the final communist stage of history or are they some kind of superhuman beings? Would man really be happy as a communist superman, or is he happier as fallible man? Be that as it may, the danger of the dialectical alternative for coping with the crisis of truth consists in its unbounded optimism and its almost religious faith in progress. This may mislead man and tempt him to regard himself as a kind of god, for whom nothing is impossible. Inspired by this optimism and by this faith, he may take up the wrong attitude to life and greatly overestimate himself. He may forget his natural limitations, lose all sense of proportion and take up an attitude which the ancient Greeks called *hubris* (a shameless pride or impudent arrogance). In this state of mind, man may easily overshoot his mark and his immodesty may be the very cause of his eventual downfall.

In our investigation of the dialectical alternative for dealing with the crisis of truth, we have so far only discussed its relationship with the functionalistic alternative, but we have not yet said anything about its relationship with the existential alternative. But if, in our discussion of the dialectical alternative, it became obvious that it divides philosophical approaches into only two kinds, namely, the materialist and the idealist approach, the conclusion can be drawn that the existential alternative is rejected by it as being idealist. And if we recall that the existential approach, so to speak, brackets the world and starts from man's being-there as a fundamental phenomenon or experience, we realize that the approaches of the dialectical and the existential alternatives must be diagonally opposed to one another.

For our purpose it will suffice if we sketch briefly the relationship that holds between the existential alternative and dialectical materialism in the light of Sartre's attempt to link up the Marxian historical materialism with existentialism. Such an attempt is made by Sartre in his work *Critique de la raison dialectique*. In this work, Sartre seeks to make existentialism the basis of historical materialism. In so doing, he hopes to combine individual freedom with the determinism of dialectical and historical materialism. "Menschen machen Geschichte auf der Basis schon gegebener Bedingungen. – Wenn diese Behauptung wahr ist, macht sie den Determinismus und die analytische Vernunft als Methode und Regel der menschlichen Geschichte endgültig hinfällig."[24] What Sartre means, therefore, is that, although man's thinking and action are conditioned by historical or social circumstances, man, nevertheless, determines history. Indeed, the problem of individual freedom in historical materialism is being hotly debated, especially among the young generation of Marxian and leftist intellectuals, who, in Germany, are greatly influenced by thinkers such as Herbert Marcuse and Ernst Bloch. The latter's monumental work *Das Prinzip Hoffnung* is branded by "orthodox" Marxians as a variation of existentialism and as a "Marxian anthropology," which conceives man as "man in

---

[24] Quoted from Adam Schaff, *Marx oder Sartre? Versuch einer Philosophie des Menschen*, p. 42.

general," instead of as "social, concrete and historical man."[25] In view of this debate, therefore, it is not surprising that Sartre's attempt at linking up existentialism with historical materialism has drawn the attention of the Marxian and leftist intellectuals as well. Sartre's suggestion to plant historical materialism on an existentialist basis is seen by the "orthodox" Marxians as undermining Marx's original doctrine and really replacing Marxism by existentialism. This is shown by the reaction of the "orthodox" Polish Marxian, Adam Schaff. He accuses Sartre of an inherent contradiction, which rests on the irreconcileability of the materialist and the existentialist approach and, therefore, leads to confusion, and he accuses Sartre of idealism. "Die These, dass die Menschen ihre Geschichte auf Grund gegebener Bedingungen machen, führt *nicht* zur Negierung des historischen Determinismus, sondern zur spezifischen Interpretation des Mechanismus, gemäss welchem dieser Determinismus arbeitet. Aber Sartre will um jeden Preis die existentialistische Auffassung der 'Freiheit' des Einzelmenschen retten. Ohne diese wäre eine 'Ergänzung' des Marxismus überflüssig... Satre spricht hier von der Dialektik der Freiheit und der Notwendigkeit, von einer Dialektik, deren äusserer Wirkung wir *unterliegen*, sowie einer Dialetik, die wir *schaffen*. All das ist schrecklich verworren und unklar, dabei aber klar in seinem Zweck."[26]

We do not see that there is so much confusion in Sartre's approach as Schaff would have it. The respective position of the two thinkers is quite clear. Sartre's starting-point remains individual man, who, by his free decision, initiates the dialectical historical process, i.e., who creates the historical and social conditions on the grounds of which he must take his future decisions. Schaff's starting-point are the historical or social conditions, which are seen as an objective dialectical process, and which determine man's consciousness and his way of acting. In other words, man remains the product of historical and social circumstances and so can only act as a member of a historical class. Schaff finds himself unable to accept Sartre's suggestion of basing historical materialism on existentialism, because, according to him, this would not, as Sartre says, deprive existentialism of its *raison d'être*, but would, on the contrary, mean the victory of existentialism over historical materialism. The basic thing, says Schaff, remains the solution of the problem of the freedom of the individual, a problem which is of fundamental significance for every existentialist. This basic idealist starting-

[25] Cf. *Geschichte der Philosophie*, ed. by the Academy of Sciences of the U. S. S. R., vol. VI, pp. 147 and 461, 462.
[26] Adam Schaff, *Marx oder Sartre? Versuch einer Philosophie des Menschen*, p. 42.

point is unacceptable to an "orthodox" Marxian philosopher, for whom man is always a product of his social surroundings and not a neutral individual that stands outside the socio-historical process. There can thus be no compromise between the standpoints of dialectical materialism and existentialism, and Sartre's attempt to bring about such a compromise, therefore, must be dismissed. "Er (Sartre) ist ja in die zwiespältige Lage eines Philosophen geraten, der den Marxismus mit dem Existentialismus in Einklang bringen will, das heisst, den marxistischen Gesichtspunkt mit dem idealistischen, genauer gesagt: dem subjektivistischen... Materialismus und Idealismus, Feuer und Wasser kann man nicht vereinen. Da hilft keine 'Dialektik'. Das Resultat ist einfach ein eklektisches Konglomerat innerer Widersprüche."[27]

In accordance with Lenin's principle of partiality (which we discussed previously), orthodox Soviet Marxism thus lays claim to being the only right interpretation of nature and of history and thus to being the only interpretation which embraces the full truth. It is, however, very questionable whether this claim has indeed been endorsed by history, especially, if we take a look at the socialist camp. At the XIV International Congress of Philosophy in Vienna, which was held at the beginning of September, 1968, the question was raised, whether, in the light of the existing crisis in the socialist camp in general and the then acute crisis in Czechoslovakia in particular, the Marxian thesis of the dialectical unity between theory and practice was still tenable. Was the Czech crisis not its clear refutation or else a violation of it, in as much as Soviet theory was applied by force to conditions in Czechoslovakia which were different from circumstances in Russia? Thus the problem arose whether the Soviet thesis that there was only one true Marxian philosophy could be maintained. Some philosophers of the socialist camp drew the conclusion that there was not one kind but several kinds of Marxism, and that the various eastern countries should be allowed to develop their own variety of Marxism in conformity with the actual circumstances of life in that particular country. These philosophers pointed out that only in this way could the unity between theory and practice be maintained.

Needless to say, the Soviet philosophers who attented the Congress of Philosophy in Vienna insisted that there was only one true Marxism. They argued that the stages socialism (as the practical application of Marxian theory) had reached in the various countries of the socialist bloc differed from one another only in degree. The oneness of the Marx-

[27] Adam Schaff, *Marx oder Sartre? Versuch einer Philosophie des Menschen*, pp. 43 and 46.

ian truth remained thereby unaffected, and the final goal was the same, namely, the absolute classless society of communism.

This led to a debate on the nature of the final goal. One Russian thinker argued that communism was not a paradisical end, but a new beginning for mankind. These conflicting views and controversial issues, however, point clearly to this: That the dialectical alternative for coping with the crisis of truth is far away from having resolved this crisis and that its projection has raised new issues, as is the case with every other truth-perspective that is developed by man in a particular existential situation. That this should be so is not surprising because the dialectical alternative is a human truth like any other. It is perspectivistic and controversial. Just as it calls in question other alternatives for coping with the crisis of truth, it is called in question by them. The truth of dialectical materialism certainly gives a valid *aspect* of reality and of human life, but it can *hardly* be the only right one among the various truth-perspectives that are developed by man from different angles and points of view and under definite existential conditions. Because these various truth-perspectives stand in a controversial relation to one another, not one of them can claim to have embraced the whole truth. This is beyond human power.

The truth of this becomes obvious if we follow the developments that took place after Lenin in Soviet Russia. Drawing the consequences from the fact that, contrary to Lenin's hopes and expectations, no socialist revolution had taken place in the west, Stalin drastically revised Marxism-Leninism and readjusted it to the fact of the continued existence of a strong capitalist West, which showed no signs of an imminent collapse. On the contrary, Soviet Marxism, after the First World War, was compelled to admit the triumph of the monopolistic form of capitalism over free capitalism. In the light of these developments, Stalin, in conformity with his thesis of socialism in one state, proclaimed the retention and the growth of the socialist state, whose functions change with internal developments inside the country and the development of the international situation. The dialectic of the socialist state was expressed in 1930 by Stalin's formula: "The highest possible development of the power of the state with the object of preparing the conditions for the dying away of the state – that is the Marxist formula."[28] This doctrine of Stalin's was contrary to Marx's and Engel's teaching that the state would gradually wither away from within, after a socialist order within the state had been established. Stalin taught

[28] Cf. Marcuse, *Soviet Marxism* "The Dialectic of the Soviet State", pp. 101-119.

that, after the victory of the revolution and progressive socialization in the Soviet Union, the class struggle would be intensified[29] and that, therefore, the process of socialization must be directed from above. It is easy to see how this doctrine enabled Stalin to entrench himself firmly as an absolute dictator and justified him in persecuting and often liquidating anyone who opposed him or was suspected of doing so. It was this theory that lurked behind the liquidation of the "capitalist" peasant class, the Kulaks, the stamping out of the "left deviationists" (Trotsky, Sinovev, Kamenev) and the "right deviationists" (Bucharin) and the purges among the army leaders in the thirties. The outcome of the Second World War strengthened Stalin's position even further. In terms of Stalinist dialectic, namely, that the internal and external policy of the state depended on internal as well as external developments, the fluctuation of Soviet foreign policy between the western allies and Germany could well be justified. And after the exclusion of Germany as a rival power after the Second World War, all the characteristics of fascism as the most virulent, oppressive and aggressive form of imperialist capitalism were transferred to America[30] as the leading imperialist power. This then was the beginning of the Cold War and the division of the world into the capitalist and the socialist bloc of powers, as we are still experiencing it to-day. In spite of all the denunciation and criticism of Stalin by contemporary Soviet philosophy as a dogmatist, who, by his subjective interpretation of Marxism-Leninism, encouraged the "cult of the person" the "objective developments" during the Stalinist era are nevertheless appreciated. Fundamentally, nothing changed after Stalin's death. The struggle for power did not fundamentally change the outlook of Soviet Marxism in regard to the nature of the state. In spite of protestations of a return to Leninism on the part of the present authorities of the Soviet Union, the Soviet state remains intact. Marcuse points out that the conflict between immediate and real interests, i.e., the conflict between individual and general interests (which Marx taught would be resolved from within the state by the working class) is now supposed to be resolved by the Soviet state as the "institutionalized collective" for the working class.[31] In the present situation of coexist-

---

[29] A thesis which in contemporary Soviet Marxism is branded as false and as serving as an excuse for Stalin's reprisals and illegal persecutions.
(cf. *Geschichte der Philosophie*, ed. by the Academy of Sciences of the U.S.S.R., vol. VI, p. 129.
[30] Cf. Marcuse, *Soviet Marxism*, p. 52.
[31] *Op. cit.*, pp. 118–119.

ence with the capitalist powers, the Soviet state is an indispensable prerequisite for bringing about the identification of immediate and real interests. While the capitalist state attempts to achieve this aim on the basis of private interests and initiative, the Soviet state endeavours to reach it on a collective basis. The dialectical relationship between economic needs and the socialist state is as follows: Whereas the improvement of economic conditions will be an indispensable presupposition for the strengthening of the socialist state, the socialist state is the prerequisite for the improvement of the economic conditions of the collective.

In his book *One-Dimensional Man*, Marcuse sees the crisis of our time, and hence the crisis of truth, in exactly this economic rivalry between the two power blocs of East and West. Each seeks to outstrip the other in the race for the above goal, naturally, in accordance with its respective economic system and method of production. It stands to reason that each power bloc has developed a managerial and technological bureaucracy, a functional apparatus and ideology in conformity with its specific structure and its specific method of trying to reach its goal. In the West, where the form of government and the social structure are determined by the private interests of the monopolists, it is the capitalist way of production (monopolies, trusts, syndicates and high finance) that determines the managerial system (industrial managers, scientists, technologists) and the ideology (philosophy, outlook of political parties). In the East, where the form of government and social structure are determined by the collective interest, it is the socialist way of production (planned production) that determines the managerial system, the functional apparatus and the ideology (philosophy and outlook of the communist party). Since, however, in the situation of sharp competition with the West, the socialist state is an absolute necessity for the planning and coordination of Soviet economy and since the communist party alone represents the right ideology in the socialist state and therefore directs its policy, it follows that all power is ultimately vested in the communist party. The party represents the proletariat as the only authentic social class, in which individual and private interests fall together. And whoever controls the party virtually controls the Soviet state, its policy, its administration and its ideology. The party, however, is controlled by its functionaries. This party bureaucracy may be seen as the new Soviet society. It, so to speak, forms the counterpart to the monopolists, bankers and financiers of the West. It stands to reason that, once firmly entrenched, the new social class of the Soviet state is reluctant to give up its privileged position and will even seek to consolidate its power further. In so doing, however, it procrastinates, if not actually prevents the full realization of socialism. For this would mean the abolition of the state, and this would in turn imply the renunciation of power by the party functionaries.

It is now against this background that Marcuse in *One-Dimensional Man* criticizes the Soviet establishment and its ideology. As we have already discussed his criticism of contemporary western thought in connection with our treatment of the functionalistic alternative for dealing with the crisis of truth, we can here concentrate on his criticism of the East. In the West, says Marcuse, the monopolists and industrial managers seek to retain their power and the monopolistic way of production as a source of this power by increasingly satisfying the material needs of their industrial slaves. By the incorporation of conflicts and contradictions into the system, these conflicts and contradictions are rendered harmless. At the same time, however, the impression of individual freedom is created; for the acceptance *on principle* of glaring and irreconcileable contradictions causes western society to become "permissive" and to tolerate almost everything. By this "permissive" policy the basic structure of the system remains unchanged, and the power of its monopolistic rulers goes unchallenged. In the East, now, the historical situation is different. Whereas western economy has to struggle with the problem of overproduction, which always threatens to plunge western economy into a new crisis, eastern economy is faced with the problem of historical backwardness.

It is on account of the historical backwardness of Soviet economy that in the eastern countries, too, there exists a discrepancy between the way of production and the productive forces. This fact furnishes the Soviet authorities with an excuse for a greater rationality (planning) of the process of industrialization and so for dictatorship, especially in a situation where eastern economy is engaged in a life and death struggle with the highly industrialized West. A state-controlled economy is the presupposition for the satisfaction of military and political needs, which must be met first in order that planning may be undertaken in such a way that the as yet unfulfilled basic needs can be met. In other words, the socialist state is to prepare the industrial slaves for freedom, and Marcuse agrees that the slaves must be free for their liberation. He points out that this was also the meaning of Marx's thesis that this liberation must be the work of the working class itself. According to

Marx, the suppression of lingering hostile tendencies within the working class by the working class itself, which takes place by necessity at the beginning, is a self-imposed necessity. Marcuse holds that the argument of historical backwardness (which he designates as the core of Soviet Marxism) has also been used by theorists of educative dictatorship from Plato to Rousseau. He seems to sympathize with the theory of Soviet Marxism that the existing contradictions between the "retarded conditions of production" and the "character of the productive forces" can be solved without an explosion, i.e., by the socialist state working in that direction with all its power, but he points out that this is only a half truth. The other half of the truth is that this mere *quantitative* change must be followed up by a *qualitative* change, namely, the disappearance of the state, the party, the plan, etc. as independent powers imposed upon individuals.

It is clear that Marcuse regards the organization of the process of production in the Soviet system as the source of the continuation of the rule of its organizers, who, in the last resort, are the highest functionaries of the communist party. This organization still separates the immediate producers (the workers) from the control of the means of production and thus causes class-distinctions. In contradistinction to the capitalist system, however, this separation is not the very motor of the process of production itself. It is not built into this process as the split of capital and labour, which has its origin in private ownership. In contradistinction to the capitalist system, the ruling social layers of the Soviet system can themselves be separated from the process of production – they are replaceable, and their replacement does not cause the overthrow of the basic social institutions.

In spite of this, Marcuse sees in this separation of the immediate producers from the control of the means of production the cause of the continued rule of the organizing classes and, for this reason, the continued enslavement of the productive class by the means of production; for they are controlled by the organizers. Marcuse's criticism of the Soviet system is directed against the present tendencies in Soviet society to delay the transition from the quantitative consolidation of socialist economy and society to qualitative change, namely, the transference of the control of the means of production from the present organizers to the immediate producers, which would lead to the withering away of the state, the dissolution of the communist party and the abolition of the present industrial and economic plan. In short, it would mean the termination of the power of the present controlling and organizing class. "In contrast to this conception, the actual development in present-day communist society postpones (or is compelled to postpone, by the international situation) the qualitative change to the second phase, and the transition from capitalism to socialism appears, in spite of the revolution, still as quantitative change. The enslavement of man by the instruments of his labor continues in a highly rationalized and vastly efficient and promising form."[32]

The question Marcuse now asks is whether the present communist system will develop the conditions for this transition to a new qualitative structure of society. He admits that there are strong arguments against such a possibility "One emphasizes the powerful resistance which the entrenched bureaucracy would offer – a resistance which finds its *raison d'être* precisely on the same grounds that impel the drive for creating the preconditions for liberation, namely, the life-and-death competition with the capitalist world."[33] Here it becomes obvious that, as a Marxian, Marcuse thinks in terms of objective historical laws and not in terms of subjective dispositions. This becomes quite clear in the following: "One can dispense with the notion of an innate 'power-drive' in human nature. This is a highly dubious psychological concept and grossly inadequate for the analysis of societal developments. The question is not whether the communist bureaucracies would 'give up' their privileged position once the level of a possible qualitative change has been reached, but whether they will be able to prevent the attainment of this level."[34] Marcuse believes that the answer to this question depends upon the world-situation, i.e., the coexistence of the two present power establishments of the East and the West. That he, however, reckons with the possibility that the historical forces will overcome the resistance of the entrenched bureaucracies of both systems transpires from the following: "The need for the all-out utilization of technical progress, and for survival by virtue of a superior standard of living may prove stronger than the resistance of the vested bureaucracies."[35]

Marcuse then thinks that neither in the capitalist systems nor in the established communist system can man's true needs really be fulfilled. In neither system can man fully realize himself, and only if this were possible would he be free and would be leading an authentic existence. In conformity with his objective view of history, therefore, Marcuse

[32] Marcuse, *One-Dimensional Man*, p. 42.
[33] *Op. cit.*, p. 44.
[34] *Op. cit.*, p. 44–45.
[35] *Op. cit.*, p. 45.

holds that the historical process ultimately aims at man's complete emancipation from all forms of open and disguised oppression, which, at present, constitute an obstacle to complete self-realization. Marcuse points out that, because of this, both the capitalist system as well as the present established communist system invite their own negation by going to extremes. On account of this, man's consciousness of the lack of freedom will be fully aroused, and man will no longer allow himself to be bound by his profession, the interests of the state and other established institutions.[36] In both systems, therefore, man will aim at the emancipation from the forces that are at present in control of the means of production and that endeavour to satisfy the material needs of their industrial slaves, each party of controlling forces doing so in accordance with its established system of production. In the West, the forces in control are motivated by private interest; in the East, they are motivated by the interest of the established socialist state and its rulers. By the striving for self-emancipation and for a qualitative change of society (i.e., a structural change) on the part of the oppressed classes of East and West, the dialectical antagonism of thesis and antithesis, which at present holds between East and West, will be resolved by a new synthesis. For the outcome will be a society, where the true individual needs are fully identified with the general interest and where the immediate producers are no longer the slaves of some manipulating forces, but organize the process of production themselves.

In order to reach this higher stage of civilization, the sciences and technology must be brought in line with the historical process. They must no longer serve the interests of a particular group or particular groups, but they must serve the interests of all men. They must become instruments of man's liberation. "Technology thus may provide the historical correction of the premature identification of Reason and Freedom, according to which man can become and remain free in the progress of self-perpetuating productivity on the basis of oppression."[37]

Marcuse points out that the contemporary technological society possesses the means in order to translate the metaphysical into the physical, the internal into the external. It is in a position to bring about the demythologization and demystification of man's metaphysical concepts, such as freedom, justice and humanity. The demystification of these concepts will not be achieved "by transferring technological omnipotence from particular groups to the new state and the central

---

[36] Marcuse, *One-Dimensional Man*, p. 45.
[37] Cf. *Op.cit.*, p. 234.

plan. Technology retains throughout its dependence on other than technological ends. The more technological rationality, freed from its exploitative features, determines social production, the more will it become dependent on political direction – on the collective effort to attain a pacified existence, with the goals which the free individuals may set for themselves."[38] In other words, demythologization and demystification will be achieved by purging technological rationality from its tendency to exploitation and subjecting it to the collective effort of all men, with a view to reaching the state of a happy existence for all. This is what Marcuse means by the *quantification of values*. Freedom, justice and humanity receive a concrete content, in as much as contemporary science and technology, if applied in the interests of all, will enable man to become free from want, despair, anxiety, suffering and conflict. There will be no more hunger, no more war from selfish motives and no more oppression of one class of men by another. The ideas of justice and humanity will so receive a concrete material content as well, and there will be general appeasement and happiness.

According to Marcuse, this historical process of man's complete economic and political emancipation by the application of the sciences and technology in the general interest leads at the same time to an increasing negation of nature. In other words, by the extension of man's control over nature, the latter is overcome in its mere naturality and is restored by the power of reason. The overcoming of nature by reason is thus also an act of freedom. The emancipatory rule of man over nature, in contradistinction to repressive rule,i.e., the rule of man over man, leads to the decrease of misery, force and cruelty. The historical process of man's increasing control over nature is a process of civilization and humanization. It goes hand in hand with the increasing emancipation of man and society and their increasing appeasement and happiness. "In Nature as well as in History, the struggle for existence is the token of scarcity, suffering, and want. They are the qualities of blind matter, of the realm of immediacy in which life passively suffers its existence. This realm is gradually mediated in the course of the historical transformation of Nature; it becomes part of the human world, and to this extent, the qualities of Nature are historical qualities. In the process of civilization, Nature ceases to be mere Nature to the degree to which the struggle of blind forces is comprehended and mastered in the light of freedom."[39]

[38] Marcuse, *One-Dimensional Man*, p. 235.
[39] *Op. cit.*, p. 236.

Marcuse, in contradistinction to the functionalistic approach with its pronounced neutralism, intends to make science and technology subservient to the historical process, the moving force of which is man's striving for the full satisfaction of material needs. Science and technology must thus be used in order to realize man's freedom in the above sense. "Consequently, what is at stake is the redefinition of values in *technical terms*, as elements in the technological process."[40] The translation of values into technological tasks means then that science and technology are no longer neutral, but are determined by these values. In this way, the theory of science, too, is radically changed. The quantified values become, so to speak, an integrated part of it, in as much as they may be said to act as the motor of the sciences and technology, as instruments by means of which man can extend more and more his control over nature. As such, they create the conditions for a happy life of full freedom and, in this sense, for man to lead an authentic existence.

It needs of course little reflection to realize that the materialization and quantification of values and their translation into technological tasks is no less functionalistic than is the neutralistic doctrine of neo-positivist philosophy. It, too, leads to a levelling of the individual by the technological process, because man's thinking will be dominated by the translation of values into technological functions, i.e., the realization of these values by science and technology. The one-sided materialization of these values leads to an overemphasis of man's material needs and the reduction of these values to the material needs, which are then regarded as basic. The question that arises is, however, whether such a reduction of human needs to a material basis in the above sense is possible or whether man's other needs, the intellectual, aesthetical and spiritual ones, exist independently of man's material needs or side by side with them. Marcuse proposes that *all* these needs will be satisfied by the further expansion of the sciences and technology in the conquest of nature and man's corresponding liberation. According to him, the spirit of enterprise and adventure as well as the free interplay of thinking and imagination assume a relational and leading part in the process of bringing out the happy existence of man and nature.[41] Faith in progress and in man's ability to shape the world and history in such a way that man is able to lead an authentic existence is the backbone of Marcuse's optimistic philosophical outlook. We ask the question,

---

[40] Cf. Marcuse, *One-Dimensional Man*, p. 232.
[41] *Op. cit.*, p.. 231 ff.

however, whether man's intellectual, aesthetical and spiritual needs can really be satisfied on such a onesided material basis. Do these various needs not differ in quality? Is man's intellectual curiosity, for instance, really based upon our desire to satisfy our material needs and to live a happy life only, or is it also (if not more so) stimulated by the wonder and puzzlement of that which we can never understand, that which we call life and death, for example, or that which we call the eternal and the infinite? If we think along these lines, it becomes very questionable whether man's intellectual curiosity can be satisfied by one definite philosophical alternative, which gives us to understand that the world and history are within the reach of man's knowledge, and that the key to this knowledge is the dialectical method. Is our aesthetical feeling only covered by the joy and happiness which we experience at having made fresh progress in the sciences and in technology or is it more? Is it, for instance, not also the pure enjoyment of a flower's beauty and the marvel such beauty arouses in us, a feeling which is absolutely free from any pragmatic note? And does not the true satisfaction of our spiritual need require the mysterious and the irrational?[42] Is this need not gratified more by that which cannot be measured, calculated and quantified and which cannot be brought under human control? The functionalism of Marcuse's method, which is an attempt to apply the teachings of Karl Marx to the contemporary situation of conflict between East and West and in this way to resolve the conflict and to show the way to the full realization of socialism in the world, differs from the functionalism of the West in method not in nature. The functionalism of the West is anti-historical. It blends man with the sciences and technology by its neutral monism, i.e., by the description of the world and of society in terms of functional structures and relations. The functionalism of Marcuse is dynamic and historical. It merges man with the sciences and technology by the quantification of values, i.e., by the translation of human values into scientific and technological functions.

From this it follows that man's freedom and happiness, and so the authentic nature of human existence, depend upon the method which is used at the constitution of the world. By the functionalistic approach of neo-positivism, man is free (from all metaphysical pathology) if he contents himself with scientific description. According to Marcuse, man

---

[42] In this regard, cf. F. M. Dostoevsky's "Legend of the Grand Inquisitor" in: *The Brothers Karamazov*. In trying to show that man is incapable of true freedom as it was demonstrated by Christ, Dostoevsky revealed great insight into man's need for the mysterious and the irrational.

is free (from the repressive forces that are in control of the means of production) if he keeps in step with history by emancipating himself from the repressive forces and assuming control over science and technology himself, with a view to the full appeasement of his material needs. It follows that man is free in neither of the two philosophical alternatives for coping with the crisis of truth; for both alternatives constitute the world by a specific method on the grounds of an adopted underlying premise, which defies experiential verification. Marcuse's quantification of values is the constitution of the world and of history by the dialectical method upon a materialist premise, namely, man's basic desire for the appeasement of his material needs. It is a new alternative for resolving the contemporary crisis of truth, which has been developed under a special aspect of the contemporary world-crisis, namely, the crisis between East and West as a scientific and technological competition between two antagonistic systems in order to satisfy the material needs of their industrial slaves. This new alternative of Marcuse's has been so designed as to overcome this crisis in theory and to end this conflict by the conception of a new form of society on a strictly material basis. It sees in the scientific and technological logos the historical logos as such. The blending of man with the historical logos results in man's absolute freedom and enables him to lead an authentic existence. As a methodological construction, however, Marcuse's new dialectical alternative for coping with the contemporary crisis of truth must be seen as a mere truth-perspective, which is controversial and, in its turn, raises new problems and new questions.

We may state the position as follows: Whereas there is much truth in Marcuse's criticism of the neo-positivist and Soviet-Marxian alternatives for coping with the crisis of truth, Marcuse's methodologically constructed or theorically conceived resolution of the crisis is no less controversial. Many questions rise in our mind. Can man really sacrifice self-interest altogether in favour of general interest (for that is what the falling together of individual interests amounts to), or is self-interest the very criterion of being human, so that the conflict between self-interest and general interest is natural and cannot be overcome by methodological constitution or, what amounts to the same, in theory only? Does not the qualitative political and social change, as envisaged by Marcuse, presuppose a qualitative change of man as well, namely, the transition from an individual to a collective being? Is such a change humanly possible, or does it lead to new dehumanization, self-estrangement and unauthenticity? In fact, the question may be asked whether, if such a change is not realizable in practice, it is brought about in theory, i.e., by the dialectical constitution of the world and of history, and, in this sense, can take place only in Marcuse's imagination. If this is true, then the question arises whether there exists in history such an objective dialectical law or logos which, by the expansion of the sciences and technology, causes man's individual consciousness to change into a collective one. Such a collective consiousness must not be confused with the neutral mind of neo-positivist thinking or with the levelling of the mind by technological functionalism and automatism. In contradistinction to this, it is an active mind, engaged in the process of its own liberation and in establishing a free and happy society. It is a free mind, which enables man to create himself in response to his natural needs and desires. Instead of being dominated by the sciences and technology, it consciously uses and directs the sciences and technology for the purpose of absolute freedom and happiness.

In our opinion, this beautiful conception is a mere utopia. By the increasing scientific and technological control of man over the world, for whatever lofty ideals, a levelling of man's mind will take place, i.e., man will eventually succumb to the functionalistic forces which he has developed, and these forces will come to rule his entire life, absorb his time and lead him to a shallow mob-thinking. It thus stands to reason that, in spite of a different approach and a different aim, the functionalistic and the dialectical alternatives for coping with the crisis of truth both have the same effect on man. Under the treatment of both these philosophical approaches, he emerges as a robot. The logical outcome of Marcuse's philosophy is thus exactly that against which he so violently fought, namely, *one-dimensional man*.

PHILOSOPHY AS A REPRESENTATION OF THE NATURE OF TRUTH

I. GENERAL OBSERVATIONS

Truth may be defined as the absolute object, which would be known as the perfectly integrated One, if such knowledge were possible. In actual fact, however, such knowledge is impossible. As should have become evident from our discussion of different philosophical alternatives for coping with the crisis of truth, truth presents itself to man in the form of various aspects, which may be described as fragments of the real. Each philosophical alternative which we investigated, the functionalistic, the existential and the dialectical one, revealed itself as a cycle of the human self. Each alternative sought to overcome man's self-estrangement and the alienation of man from the world or from being and, in so doing, tried to restore the authentic character of human existence by the methodological constitution of the world or of being from a definite starting-point and from a specific underlying assumption or premise. It became obvious, however, from our discussions that none of the proposed philosophical alternatives for coping with the crisis of truth succeeded in dealing with it in such a way as to overcome it. On the contrary, the insistence of each alternative on its holding alone the key to the resolution of the crisis and so being in possession of *the* truth has only sharpened the crisis to such an extent that another catastrophe seems imminent.

The very fact that these various philosophical alternatives have been developed in answer to the same crisis and by their uncompromising opposition to one another have even sharpened it, raises the question whether any human truth of whatever nature, scientific, historical, philosophical or theological, will ever be able to resolve the crisis of human truth, and whether it is not the very nature of human truth to be for ever in a critical stage or to be constantly called in question. If, however, the critical character of the human logoi is something that is natural, something that issues from man's very finiteness and changeableness, the question should be asked whether the crisis of human truth should not be accepted as something that is congenial to man, instead of being regarded as something that is foreign to him and that must be overcome at any cost. We may also formulate our question as follows: Is not the permanent crisis in which human truths find themselves the *sufficient reason* for the question about truth to be asked again and again by philosophy? Is this crisis not the very motor of human thought and action? Is it not the very ground for the continual creation and recreation of our cultural values and goods of civilization? If this is so, then human truth, culture and civilization are forever changing, and man is forever on the way. He is by nature a historical being, who, by continually projecting himself into the world under specific circumstances of life, creates ever new existential situations, with which he has to cope afresh by the projection of ever new philosophical alternatives. It is obvious that, by projecting himself into the world, man inevitably enters into controversy with his fellowman; for he is the one who reacts to man's philosophical project by positing his own project from his own existential situation and thus from his own point of view. The same process goes on in the other fields of culture and civilization, in the sciences, in history and in theology, for example. It is in this way that the various fields of culture and civilization have developed and that they are undergoing constant change. Every methodological constitution in these various fields of human activity created new problems and caused new perspectives to be developed. As a result of the controversial character of the human truth-perspectives in the various fields of human culture, therefore, the historical nature of human truth in general becomes obvious. As now the question about truth in general is asked by philosophy, philosophical systems and projects may be regarded as attempts to answer this question in the light of the particular circumstances of the times. The historical nature of human truth can thus best be examined if we are aware of the historical nature of philosophy.

2. THE HISTORICAL NATURE OF PHILOSOPHY

When studying philosophy, we are at once struck by the great number and variety of philosophical systems and projects that were developed throughout the centuries of human history. The questions that arise are the following: What is the cause of this great number of philosophical systems? Why is there no homogeneous philosophy? Why do philosophical thinkers fail to arrive at conclusions of general validity, so that philosophy still lacks the final answer? These questions throw light upon the nature of philosophy and hence upon the nature of human truth. What really is philosophy? What is its purpose and what is its field of investigation?

It is generally known that it is impossible to give an adequate definition of philosophy, as every definition is at once problematic again. This is proved by the many various definitions that have been attempted. When we ask the question: What is philosophy?, we are already philosophizing. Why is that so? We believe that this is due to philosophy's asking questions in a *universal* manner. The fundamental question asked by philosophy appears to be the question about truth in general. The individual sciences, which originally developed from philosophy, so to speak, relativized this question, i.e., they reduced it to apply to a circumscribed material or content. Thus physics and chemistry, for example, confined their investigations to the inorganic world of things, biology concentrated upon the world of living organisms and history examined human actions in the past. Theology (at least in its proper domain) explored forms of faith and the relations of man to the deity. This restriction to a circumscribed field of investigation made it easier to draw general conclusions on matters in a particular sphere than was possible in the case of philosophy. This held true especially in the natural sciences, which, unlike history, examined things and not human behaviour, which is often difficult to account for. But even in the natural sciences, the general validity of natural laws and scientific theories is really relative and of limited duration. It only lasts as long as, by experimentation, new phenomena are discovered (or as long as, by experimentation, we have brought things to function in a new way). Also, there is no unanimous agreement about scientific theories either; every theory has its opposite number. Again and again, new aspects emerge, which lead to the formulation of new scientific concepts or to a change in meaning of the old concepts. Atom, substance, causality, energy, mass, matter and motion, to mention a few, mean something different to-day from what they meant about a hundred years ago, and what is more, these concepts are highly controversial and give rise to a great number of philosophical questions.[1]

---

[1] A good impression of this is gained by *On Modern Physics*, which contains lectures by Werner Heisenberg, Max Born, Erwin Schrödinger and Pierre Auger.

The constitutive nature of scientific truth, which renders it as problematic and historical as any other human truth, becomes also evident from the new concept of space and time. Whereas the mathematician Karl Friedrich Gauss still held that one had to admit in all humility that space had a reality outside our mind as well, to which we could not prescribe its laws *a priori*, the theory of relativity denied the concreteness of space and time. But the perspectivistic and constitutive nature of the new conception of space and time becomes clear at once when Max Planck writes in *Vom Relativen zum Absoluten* that by the new conception of space and time "ist derselbe nicht aus der Welt geschafft, sondern er ist nur weiter rückwärts verlegt worden und zwar in die Metrik der vierdimensionalen Mannigfaltigkeit, welche daraus entsteht, dass Raum und Zeit mittels Lichtgeschwindigkeit zu einem einheitlichen (vierdimensionalen) Kontinuum zusammengeschweisst werden." By the theoretical fusion of space and time into space-time, problems such as absoluteness and relativity, infinity and finiteness, continuity and discontinuity are *theoretically* solved. The world-view of the Theory of Relativity was however called in question again, e.g., by the British astro-physicist and astronomer Fred Hoyle in his *The Nature of the Universe* and *Frontiers of Astronomy*. But it stands to reason that Fred Hoyle's perspective of the constant creation of matter and his conception of a stationary condition of the world are being called in question again.[2]

Whereas the scientist, again and again, comes forth with new scientific theories, views on nature and even cosmologies, which include man and explain human culture and civilization in terms of natural or cosmological laws, the historian proper, again and again, systematically explores the events of the past and methodologically constitutes them or interprets them in agreement with the changing *Zeitgeist*. It is the *Zeitgeist* or the call of the time which determines the prevailing interests and the kind of questioning of historians.[3] No matter how objective

[2] In regard to the perspectivistic nature of human truth and hence also scientific truth, cf. Erwin Schrödinger, *Meine Weltansicht*, although we do not agree with his metaphysical ideal (which he takes from Indian Philosophy and from Albert Schweitzer) that all living beings are various aspects of one being, which we call God and the Hindus Brahma. In reference to the subjective aspect in scientific thinking, Schrödinger says "Schon eine vollkommen sichere, unzweideutige Verständigung der Menschen untereinander ist unmöglich, ist ein Ziel, dem wir uns immer mehr nähern, das wir aber nie erreichen können. *Schon aus eiesem Grunde ist exakte Wissenschaft nie wirklich möglich*". p. 116.

[3] The same applies to scientists or theologians. They, too, can never ask exactly the same kind of questions as did their predecessors, because the scientific or theological projects of their predecessors raised new questions and opened new vistas and perspectives. It is on account of this that the various cultural are fields in a permanent state of becomnig.

a historian strives to be, he can never perfectly comply with Leopold von Ranke's demand that historical events must be treated exactly as they happened at the time. The historian cannot step outside his own time, and he cannot ignore the influence of his environment, e.g., the tradition in which he is steeped, the particular interests he pursues, the value to which he subscribes; and even the "modern" methods which he applies in his investigations are the product of his own age. The medieval Christian historian, for example, judged history and culture differently from the historian of more recent times, say, the historian of the Enlightenment era. And even in the presentation of history by contemporary historians, there are fundamental differences, as is shown by the completely different approach to history of the historians of the West and the historians of the East. While the former cannot help reading history in the light of the liberalistic and humanitarian values to which they subscribe, the latter are committed to read history in terms of historical materialism.

The differences become yet more outspoken when it comes to the philosophy of history. Augustine, Hegel, Marx, Burckhardt, Toynbee, Popper, to mention a few philosophers of history, put forward doctrines in which the spirit of their age is clearly manifested. Kurt Breysig, who sees the meaning of all historical enquiry in untwining the rope of history, i.e., undoing the web of time that is woven by historical events, emphasizes the point that historical research does not stand above or outside history, but is itself interwoven in the web of time. History is thus made and experienced by man. Giving an account of history, always means to man giving an account of himself.[4]

In each case, in that of the natural sciences and in that of history, the question about truth depends upon a definite way of questioning and upon a definite method of enquiry. It is then always man who, in continual exchange of opinions, ideas, views, hypotheses and theories and thus in continual controversy with his fellowman and his colleague methodologically constitutes the world and the past and gets them under his control by rational comprehension.

Exactly the same happens in philosophy, except that the field of enquiry of philosophy is universal because the question about truth is asked by philosophy on a general level. Philosophy, then, does not distinguish itself *fundamentally* from the individual sciences, but merely by the comprehensiveness of its field of enquiry. It has that in common with the individual sciences that it develops its answers to the ques-

---

[4] Cf. K. Breysig, *Meister der entwickelnden Geschichtsforschung.*

tion about truth systematically and methodologically, in accordance with the particular circumstances of life and man's vital interest in a specific epoch. The philosophical systems or alternatives for dealing with the problem of truth that have been projected into the world throughout the centuries are relative in a double respect. In the first place, they refer to a definite historical period, the problems and conflicts of which they reflect; in the second place, they refer to another system or alternative, which had previously been constructed and which they call in question, only to be called in question themselves by new systems or projects, which are posited in answer to them.

As a result of the historical character of the philosophical systems or alternatives posited as methodological projects by man from an actual contingent situation (systems or alternatives which call each other in question), we gain insight into the nature of philosophy and hence into the nature of human truth. Philosophy is historical in that it asks the question about *the* truth from the actual historical process or the process of becoming itself, i.e., on the basis of the continually changing needs and interests of man. It is historical in that it answers this question in an ever new way, in accordance with the prevailing conflicts or problems , in short, with the particular crisis or existential situation as man experiences it at any particular stage. Philosophy projects its alternatives in a systematic or methodological form. It orders and arranges man's surroundings by trying to develop a meaningful world-view, which serves man as a guide in his particular existential situation and under the specific conditions of the time in which he lives. From philosophy's historical, periodical and finite nature in the above sense, it follows that the question about *the* truth must be asked again and again, and that the world must be ordered und arranged in an ever new form, as the circumstances of life change. Philosophy, therefore, like all the other sciences, is in a permanent process of becoming. It can never be static and one-dimensional. As representing man's constant endeavour to find out about the truth, it can never be a closed system, but is by nature an open science, which records man's actual experience of the world at a particular historical stage.

To call philosophical activity a *scandal* because of its failure to achieve knowledge, the evidence of which is recognised by all philosophers, is to misunderstand of the nature of philosophy. If there were evidence to which all philosophers agreed, man would stop philosophizing. In that case, however, he would no longer be man either, but would know *the* truth and be like God, or he would cease to exist and

be nothing. It is precisely when we take man as man, with all his aspirations, needs, interests, weaknesses, shortcomings and failures that
we begin to understand the nature and purpose of philosophy as well
as man's continual philosophical and cultural activities throughout
history. After all, philosophy, as all the other individual sciences, is
man's creation and, as such, reflects man's limitation and inadequacy.
In however absolute or universal a form man may ask his question
about truth, the answer he receives to his question by his systematic
exploration and methodological constitution of the material and intellectual world is always perspectivistic and controversial. It is always
in a critical stage because it calls in question other philosophical truth-
perspectives and is in turn called in question itself. Man's perspectivistic limitation, on account of man's finite and shifting nature, explains
the historical limitation of philosophy as being in a permanent process
of becoming; for it is due to the perspectivistic character of the human
logoi that these logoi are referred to each other in controversy, so finding themselves in a permanent crisis, which man and his fellowmen
experience in common as their mutual limitation. It is the permanent
question about truth under continually changing circumstances of life,
or else the continual controversy between man and his fellowmen in
their common quest for truth that keeps in progress the process of
culture and civilization. If then philosophy, by its universal way of
posing the question about truth, arrived at general conclusions of absolute validity, i.e., if it could really answer the question about *the* truth,
it would abolish itself. All problems and conflicts would be solved, and
all further philosophizing would be superfluous. At this stage, nothing
would happen anymore; for the continual controversy about truth
that goes on between man and his fellowman would be over. This
would then mean that the process of culture and civilization, and thus
the process of history, would come to a standstill.

From this it becomes clear that the crisis of human truth is something
that is inherent in human nature itself. It is then futile to try to overcome this crisis, and it is reasonable to accept it as the very ground of
human culture and civilization and thus of history. If, now, the philo-
lophical alternatives that deal with the present crisis of truth, the
functionalist, existential and dialectical alternative, claim to have overcome it, there is something essentially wrong. They can be said to have
done so only in their imagination or in theory, i.e., by the methodological constitution of a scientific, a mystical and a historical logos respectively, which they regard as absolute and in terms of which man is

supposed to be re-housed and to recover his authentic existence, i.e., his existence in freedom. In reality, however, man, by each of these alternatives, is led away from his actual experience and secludes himself in the *cycle of his own self*. This happens because the constitution of any absolute logos of whatever kind, from whatever premise, is nothing but a theoretical conception of an immanent truth, which is systematically or methodologically developed. The dangers that lurk in this self-seclusion of man and the negative effect it has in respect to his relationship with others, due to a closed mind, are obvious. By believing himself to be in possession of *the* truth, man becomes dogmatic, intolerant and fanatical. He will keep chasing a phantom, which will forever slip away from him. Philosophy cannot embrace *the* truth, as becomes evident from the controversial character of any projects or alternatives for coping with the problem of truth. Only if the basic experience of the crisis of our truth is heeded, can man be freed or, rather, can he set himself free from the prison of his own truth, which he so diligently keeps constructing for himself. Only then can he break through the cycle of his own self and turn from the immanent to the emanent, from the theoretical to the practical.

In order to become aware of the real nature of human truth, therefore, we must stop regarding philosophy as one closed system or as one definite method, which is based on a certain underlying premise. That philosophy is a closed system or a definite method is proved wrong by our keen experience of the contemporary crisis of truth, which issues from the total character and the total confrontation with one another of the contemporary philosophical alternatives for coping with the crisis. The fact, however, that the crisis has become so acute that it points to a new catastrophe, which is about to befall us, shows how controversial the contemporary philosophical alternatives really are. The catastrophe that might result from the total clash of these alternatives can be avoided only if the crisis itself is accepted as the *sufficient reason* for all human thinking and for all human truth and if, thereby, the finite, temporal and historical nature of philosophy or of human truth is fully recognized, and if man draws the appropriate conclusions from this insight and behaves and acts accordingly. In other words, man must learn to regard philosophy as his mirror, which reflects his true nature, i.e., his limitation, his historicity, his temporality, his being bound up with the existential situation in which he finds himself, etc.. If philosophy is regarded in this way, its true nature will be understood. It now reveals itself as a critical science, the permanent critical situation of which clearly shows the limit of human knowledge and leads to self-critical insight and wise self-restriction on man's part, instead of rousing in him the idea that he is a mortal god.

3. THE ANTHROPOLOGICAL CHARACTER OF PHILOSOPHICAL PROJECTS

If philosophy is regarded as man's mirror and as revealing the real nature of human truth, its anthropological character becomes clearly manifest. In the philosophical systems, as they were projected into the world in accordance with the particular circumstances of the time, man's prevailing needs and interests, the specific conflicts with which he had to wrestle were reflected. It does not matter what oppositional pair of philosophers we take: Plato and Aristotle; Thomas Aquinas and William Occam; Descartes and Locke; Kant and Fichte; Hegel and Marx; Wittgenstein and Heidegger. In each case, these philosophers develop their methods in a particular existential situation, under the particular tensions, conflicts and needs of a specific epoch. Always, they stand in a controversial relation to one another, and, always, they provoke new contradiction. The philosophical projects or alternatives for coping with the crisis of truth, under specific existential circumstances and in a specific climate of life, disclose man's continual struggle about the truth, which, as such, remains inaccessible and, as human truth, is in a constant flux. Again and again, man must constitute the truth, so as to keep in step with the actual historical processes or else to respond to his actual contingent experience of the permanent crisis of all human truth. By reason of the continual controversy between man and his fellowmen, man projects himself into the world in ever new forms. He proceeds from one manner of questioning to another, so discovering ever new perspectives and dimensions of truth.

The progressive constitution of truth in an ever new form in the field of the permanent crisis which holds between man and the other, the I and the thou, or else between their truth-perspectives (a constitution which is the meaningful rearrangement of the world by the philosophical system or the philosophical method) causes all philosophical projects to become immanent truths or *cycles of the human self*. This also holds true if the transcendent is conceived as standing in a dialectical relationship with the world, as was for instance the case in the existential alternative for coping with the crisis of truth. For this dialectical relationship is rationally comprehended, and, in this way, the actual contradiction between immanent and emanent is removed. By the rational comprehension of the dialectical relationship, contradictories are subsumed under the law of identity.

The anthropological character of the philosophical alternatives for coping with the crisis of truth becomes even more pronounced if we keep in mind that human self-projection into the world in an ever new form happens as a result of man's existential wants and needs. These needs were described by us as being of a material, intellectual, aesthetical and spiritual kind. It is they that lend truth its value character. Because of his experience of being constantly called in question and owing to the constant threat to his existence by the other, man, in every respect, strives for the greatest possible certainty and security. In this sense, we may also understand the words of Francis Bacon: "Scientia potentia est" or "natura parendo vincitur."

The attempt to control his environment with the aim of making life as pleasant as possible, the desire for knowledge, the striving for an understanding of himself or his own nature and the yearning for the transcendent must be traced to the existential root of man's feeling of uncertainty and insecurity. This feeling grows out of the permanent crisis in which man finds himself with the other, man's permanent stumbling block. It is this existential root of man's life that causes man to order and arrange his sourroundings in an ever new form and to subject them to his systematic control, i.e., to understand and grasp them in a rational manner and, by so doing, dispose of them in his interest. By the philosophical constitution of the world, the world is, so to speak, humanized or civilized, even by being subjected to human control. By whatever method such constitution of the world takes place, the positive or the negative, the constructive or the critical, in each case the constitution of the world by man is an act of man's self-projection in the world in an ever new form, on the grounds of life's changed or changing circumstances. It is now precisely by this act of man's continual self-projection in the world in the form of philosophical alternatives for coping with man's changing existential conditions and in the form of the individual sciences and technology that the process of culture and civilization is kept in progress.

4. THE SYSTEMATIC ASPECT OF THE HISTORY
OF PHILOSOPHY AS THE MIRROR OF HUMAN TRUTH

A. The Logic of the History of Philosophy

We observed that the historical philosophical alternatives were referred to one another in controversy and that they call each other in question. If this is the case, none of the alternatives can lay claim to representing *the* truth, but these alternatives always represent only a relative truth. Now, since all philosophical systems or alternatives are posited in the name of *the* truth, it follows that truth shows itself to us as the non-comprehension of the absolute truth. The truth that reveals itself in the controversial relation that obtains between human truths leads to a *docta ignorantia*, which possesses universal validity. Whereas there are as many human truths as there are philosophical and scientific methods, which constantly change, the truth of our non-comprehension of *the* truth is of a permanent and universal kind.

The controversial relation that holds between human logoi or the permanent crisis-situation in which human truths find themselves leads to a *critical logic*, which, nonetheless, has positive implications. *The* logos, so to speak, dawns as a multiple logos in the controversial relation that exists between human truths. For in the light of *the* truth, in the name of which they are posited, the human logoi are referred and are complementary to one another.

From the crisis-situation of the human logoi, on the grounds of which they are referred to one another and in which *the* logos emerges as a *docta ignorantia*, as the truth of the non-comprehension of *the* truth, man's reasonable thinking and acting become clear. Such reasonable thinking rests upon man's awareness of the perspectivistic and critical nature of human truth, which, in its limitation and completeness, requires supplementation by other perspectives and dimensions of truth. A good example to demonstrate this point is the empirical and the rational approach of constituting philosophical truth. Both constitutions are true only in as much as they represent the rational development of specific premises by various methods. On the one hand, a start is made from the premise of sense-perceptions, and one seeks to arrive at general results by the *inductive method* and the synthetic judgement. On the other hand, the starting-point is reason itself, from which premise one attempts to determine the structure of the world and man's nature by the *deductive method* and the analytical judgment. Obviously, both methods require supplementation, and no less a thinker than Immanuel Kant sought to reconcile them by the *transcendental method* and by his discovery of the synthetical judgment *a priori*. But, obviously, Kant could not exhaust all dimensions of truth either, and was called in question in his turn by other thinkers. Fichte, Schelling and Hegel, but also Schopenhauer and much later Jaspers, developed his thinking further and, in their turn, raised new problems and gave rise to new controversy, in this way opening the way for new vistas or the exploration of new dimensions of truth. From this it follows that the reasonable act consists in accepting the criticism or the calling in question of one's own truth by others. For only in the positive controversy and exchange of ideas with the other, can my own truth be corrected or supplemented and vice versa, so that it becomes beneficial not only to myself, but to the other as well.

Generally speaking, the logical character of the controversial relation that obtains between two human logoi consists in this that it refers my own truth to that of the other. Thereby the logical function of the historical philosophical alternatives for coping with the crisis of truth is clearly outlined. Positively speaking, this function consists in the meaningful arrangement and ordering of the environment from a particular existential situation. Negatively speaking, the logical function of the historical philosophical alternatives leads to a *docta ignorantia*, i.e., the revelation of the truth of the non-comprehension by man of *the* truth, whereby the many various philosophical logoi are related to one another in truth.

This clearly reveals the crisis-situation in which human truth constantly finds itself as the *ratio sufficiens* of all human truth, whereby its historical nature is explained. From this actual experience of the permanent crisis of human truth, which is shared by man and his fellowman in common and by which man and his fellowman are referred to one another, it follows that all theoretically conceived or constituted reasons or grounds of truth are ipso facto controversial. And if, as appears to be the case with the contemporary alternatives for coping with the crisis of truth, these reasons or grounds are conceived as universally valid and, in this sense, as absolute, it follows that this involves a logical contradiction; for how can the reasons and grounds of philosophical alternatives possibly be of universal validity or absolute if these alternatives are themselves historical and are referred to one another in controversy? The conception of these truth-perspectives as universally valid is therefore unreasonable. We must thus not be surprised if the action of those who insist upon the universality and absoluteness of the respective truth-perspective to which they subscribe is unreasonable as well.

To conclude this brief logic of the history of philosophy, we will say this: If the crisis-situation in which human truths find themselves, or else the controversial relation by which human logoi are referred to one another, is realized as being the *ratio sufficiens* of all human truth and the cause of the historical character of all human truth (in the sense of human truth being in a constant process of becoming), the constitution of a functionalistic, a mystical and a dialectical logos (as this is found to be the case with the functionalistic, the existential and dialectical alternative respectively) is illogical. Such mere theoretical conception misleads man and guides him away from his actual experience. It causes him to worship progress and to fix his gaze at a dream-world of perfect harmony and integrity, with the object of blending with it in some way or other. By so doing, he hopes to achieve happiness and peace of mind. It is his imagination of being linked in some way or other with absolute truth through his constitutive effort which makes him act unreasonably towards his fellowman, with whom he is in reality related in controversy and with whom, therefore, he should cooperate on the grounds of the crisis which he shares with him, instead of trying to overcome this situation by theoretical conception and construction.

B. *The Epistemology of the History of Philosophy*

The logical character of the history of philosophy consists in the continual meaningful rearrangement of man's environment by the existentially conditioned philosophical alternatives and in the reasonable relationship established between these alternatives on the grounds of the permanent crisis in which they find themselves with one another. It was in fact by the continual question about truth on account of this permanent crisis that new dimensions of truth were discovered. The epistemological character of the history of philosophy consists above all in its *empirical limit*, which becomes clearly marked by the controversial relation which obtains between the philosophical projects. For this relation is actually experienced by man and his fellowman in common as the crisis of their respective truth, which is being called in question by the other. It thus stands to reason that we have no knowledge beyond this empirical limit, or else that if we transcend this limit by positing our own one-sided truth in an absolute manner, we do so at the expense of other truth-perspectives, and we block the way towards the discovery of new dimensions of truth. The real unfolding of truth and the real progress of culture and civilization takes place, as we have observed, by controversy. Just as, therefore, the experience of the actual crisis of our truth proved the sufficient reason of the continual projection into the world of truth-perspectives in an ever new manner, so this same experience also reveals itself as the sufficient reason of our knowledge. Just as human truth revealed itself as historical, so human knowledge shows its historical character. That this is true is not surprising if we realize that human knowledge is actually nothing but the functional character of human truth. By that is meant that knowledge is that which has been methodologically constituted in the sciences, in history, in philosophy and in theology. There is thus not one kind of knowledge, but there are several kinds, and, moreover, the nature of our knowledge changes, as do the manner of our questioning and the methods of our enquiry. As far as our enquiry into nature is concerned, the original question that was asked was: What is a thing? What is its essence? The method in order to establish the essence of a thing was that of the analytical judgment. It was not until the 16th and 17th centuries that this question began to be replaced by the question: How does a thing function? Thus, gradually, the qualitative approach came to be replaced by the quantitative approach, and the analytical judgment was superseded by the synthetical judgment. Properties of things were no longer regarded as essence, but as processes, which could be measured and the measurement of which could be laid down in terms of mathematics. As Galileo put it: "The great book of nature lies open before us. In order to be able to read it, we need mathematics, for it is written in mathematical language. Natural events are quantitative and thus measureable. Where this is not immediately the case, science must arrange the experiment in such a way that they become measurable." The cause and effect relation was no longer explained in terms of the Aristotelian *potentia* and *actualitas*, which pointed to an inherent vital force or idea as the forming principle (*entelechaia*), but it was now restricted to measurable processes. What had to be sacrificed, however, was the element of logical necessity and hence of certainty, which was replaced by contingency and probability.

If in the light of this development the question were asked whether, by the new approach, our knowledge of nature has increased, the answer would be this: If by knowledge is meant our knowledge of what a thing is, or, more accurately, what its essence is, the answer would be, no. If, however, by knowledge is meant our familiarity with how things function or our ability to make them function, so that we can use them for our purpose and make them serviceable to our material needs, the answer would be, yes. In other words, our knowledge has increased in as much as our functional skill has improved, i.e., in as much as our scientific methods have extended our control over our surroundings and increased our power of penetration into the past in the science of history. For it is we who, through our scientific methods, make things function and constitute the past in various forms and, in this way, dispose of them. It is for this reason that we designated knowledge as the functional character of truth; for it may be said that we know only that which we have constituted ourselves.

If, however, what we constitute ourselves is always questionable and controversial, our knowledge is characterized by the same criteria as well. If absolute truth is outside our ken, universal knowledge is as impossible. To pretend that universal knowledge is possible, as in fact is done by all the contemporary philosophical alternatives for dealing with the crisis of truth (even though universal knowledge may not mean the same thing in each particular case; for what is meant by this expression depends on the the specific method used by a particular alternative), is thus to mislead man. Such a claim must cause him to misjudge his true nature and to overrate his capacity and ability to such an extent that he may develop an attitude of *hubris*, which may eventually bring about his downfall. Let us not overlook the fact that the improvement of our functional skill, and hence of our knowledge, has also a negative side. Not only has man's destructive power increased thereby to such an extent that he is in a position to blot out mankind altogether, so that all knowledge would cease anyhow, because there would be no knower anymore, but even where man has put his functional skill to positive use, fresh problems emerge. For instance, the lowering of the death-rate among babies and the extension of man's span of life through the scientific achievements in medicine aggravated the problems of overpopulation and nutrition. In this way, it becomes clear that man is compelled to direct and redirect his functional skill so as to be able to cope with ever new problems, which emerge as the very result of his scientific achievements; and there appears to be no end to this process. Everything man does is, after all, only patch-work, however astounding and admirable his functional accomplishments may be. Man stops one hole, only to find that another hole appears. Being himself subject to the processes and events of nature, man cannot possibly step outside nature and establish his absolute rule over it. No matter how far he will advance in gaining functional control over nature, there will always be a fresh barrier, a fresh obstacle in the way, apart from the fact that, in the end, no matter in how many million years, nature is bound to overcome man. Just like man, the earth and our whole solar system are doomed to die, so that organic life will cease to exist. If nature so pleased, man's end could also come suddenly, for instance, by a huge meteor or comet crashing into the earth, upsetting all our carefully constructed "laws of nature." The worst negative effect of the tremendous and astonishing improvement of man's functional skill is the construction by man of an artifical world of science and technology, which man mistakes for reality and the prisoner of which he becomes to an ever increasing extent. We came across this problem when dealing with the functionalistic approach and the levelling and brainwashing effect this approach had on man, and we came across it again when we discussed the effect on man of Marcuse's doctrine of the quantification of values.

In the light of the above, it becomes very important for man to realize the historical and controversial nature of his knowledge, as it is so aptly illustrated throughout the history of philosophy, and as it is demonstrated to-day by the controversy over the nature of knowledge, which is in progress among the philosophisal alternatives that seek to cope with the current crisis of truth. Thus in the case of the functionalistic alternative, knowledge may be said to consist in the description of man and the world in terms of scientific or ordinary language. In the event of the existential alternative, knowledge may be said to consist in man's intuition or his being-there as the manifestation of being or else the nothing. In the case of the dialectical alternative, knowledge consists in the dialectical motion of matter. It is obvious that, in each of these philosophical alternatives, a claim is laid to the infallibility of knowledge, in accordance with the respective underlying premise upon which this knowledge is based. The fact, however, that these philosophical projects stand in a controversial relation with one another, again reveals the crisis-situation as the empirical limit of our knowledge. In other words, our knowledge can only be called real and true if we remain conscious of its essentially controversial character, which can never be overcome by analysis, intuition or dialectic; for they are themselves methods of the constitution of our knowledge.

Whatever starting-point the philosopher may choose to adopt in developing his philosophical project, the realistic or the idealistic, the empirical or the rationalistic, the analytical, dialectical or existential one, he will always experience the limit of his knowledge by the crisis in which he finds himself with the other and in which both are referred to one another. By this experience, the philosopher is always referred to the field of actual experience. It is this field that outlines itself as the ground of common action between man and his fellowman. On this ground, both find themselves in continual controversy with one another, thus fighting the permanent battle about truth. It is in this way that the conception of ever new ideas and the creation of ever new values of culture and goods of civilization takes place. The empirical limit, however, which is so keenly experienced in this process and which is so clearly manifest when we study the history of philosophy, teaches at the same time the inaccessibility to man of *the* truth. It is now exactly this *real* transcendence of *the* truth which makes man remain in constant quest for it and which spurs him on to ever new achievements in the field of culture and civilization.

By the permanent crisis in which the philosophical systems find themselves on account of their constantly calling each other in question, the critical character of philosophy is revealed as well. The empirical limit refers and confines philosophy to the field of man's actual experience, the field that is common to all men. As a critical science, which is conscious of its changing controversial and finite character, philosophy should make an effort to conceive a new meaningful worldview and new norms and values of life in accordance with the prevailing circumstances of our age, which will serve man as a guide and by which he can orientate himself in the actual crisis in which he finds himself. Being fully conscious of its historical character, philosophy should always keep itself open for the changing circumstances of life and the prevailing *Zeitgeist*. It should not become a closed fossilized dogmatic system or method, as, we are afraid, is the case with the contemporary philosophical projects seeking to master the current crisis of truth. To put it otherwise, philosophy must order and arrange man's world meaningfully, in accordance with the particular existential situation in which man happens to find himself and in accordance with the particular needs as they arise in his specific situation. Only in this way, can philosophy remain in step with reality and will it enable man to live a life in accordance with his true nature as an essentially historical and controversial being. Philosophy should thus state nothing about the transcendent, which is beyond human experience and therefore human knowledge.

It should leave statements of this nature to theology, which, on the basis of revelation and faith, is able to report on the transcendent.

C. *The Metaphysics of the History of Philosophy*

The philosophical alternatives for coping with the contemporay crisis of truth each lay claim to being anti-metaphysical. It is true that they no longer consciously constitute an absolute, as was the case in classical metaphysics. By laying claim, however, to the universal validity of their respective vision of truth, they cannot avoid being metaphysical, for, in so doing, they transcend the empirical limit, as it emerges from our actual experience. In conformity with their underlying premise and their method of developing this premise in a rational manner, they constitute a universal logos, in terms of which the structure of the world is explained and the authenticity of man's existence is determined. In accordance with the principle of identity, the contemporary philosophical projects that try to master the current crisis of truth identify man's ego or consciousness with the universe. They do this by constituting the universe methodologically and, in this manner, grasping it as an immanent absolute truth, no matter how "objective" or "neutral" they imagine their truth to be.

The functionalistic alternative, for instance, constitutes the world by the descriptive or analytical method. By tracing the functional calculus of scientific or ordinary language propositions, it comprehends man, the world and the contrasts within the world in terms of the functional relations that exist among these propositions. What happens in the functionalistic approach is that the concepts about the world lose their first order position and become second order concepts. Energy, matter, substance, causality, space, time, reality, self, mind, spirit, soul, intellect, will, etc. do no longer denote things or phenomena directly or essences behind processes or phenomena, but they stand for certain processes or for the specific behaviour of natural phenomena or of man. In this way, qualities or properties have become quantified, and these processes are described in terms of the functional relations of words and propositions. It may thus be said that these functional relations become the essence of the world. As truth-functions, they lend the world a rational character by which the world becomes constituted in a meaningful way; and in terms of the functionalistic method this truth is of a universal nature.

That the claim to neutrality by the functionalistic method is untenable becomes obvious from its methodological character. Any method of understanding the world, whether descriptive or explanatory, is constitutive; any method presupposes a theory *about* the world and *about* language, no matter how much this is denied.[5] Any kind of methodological or systematic interpretation of the world, therefore, presupposes a subject or consciousness which establishes the premise and develops it rationally and logically. Any kind of method is a self-projection of man in the world, whereby it becomes his world and thus an immanent truth. By the methodological constitution of the world in the sense of ordering it meaningfully on the basis of a specific historical situation, therefore, man keeps moving within the cycle of his own self. And we have already observed in our discussion of the functionalistic alternative for dealing with the crisis of truth that this alternative links up with other historical alternatives and that it, too, has really been projected on the grounds of particular historical circumstances or of definite problems and conflicts which it seeks to solve. We observed that it does so by blending man with the world through the descriptive method. This was criticized and opposed by other thinkers. To this criticism, we wish to add that, by the constitution of a universal functionalistic logos, the functionalistic alternative transcends the empirical limit of man's actual contingent experience and, by this self-transcendence on man's part, becomes metaphysical.

The existential alternative interprets the world in the light of man's being-there. Seen in the light of this premise, the world becomes something that is hostile to man, something into which he is thrown as a stranger. The existential alternative, therefore, constitutes being in terms of nothing, i.e., it recognizes being in man's being-there as a being-to-nothing. In the existential alternative, nature is excluded, and being or the absolute manifests itself in man's very historicity, periodicity and finiteness, in his very failure to comprehend being and in the border-situations in which he constantly finds himself. In other words, the existential method makes the jump into the transcendent inevitable, just because the absolute is unknown. If in classical metaphysics being or the absolute was a definite something that was conceived as the reason of all that exists, being or the absolute is now the unknown which manifests itself in man's very finiteness and temporality, and in his inability to comprehend it.

But in spite of this reversal, which causes the existential philosophers to think against classical metaphysics, the dialectical relationship between man and the absolute remains. The absolute remains the dialec-

---

[5] Cf. E. Gellner, *Words and Things*.

tical other of human subjectivity, with which this other is reconciled in thought. For thinking *possesses* an object or is directed towards something which is always the other of thinking. But the word "possess" indicates the constitutive character of this other in thought. Already Eberhard Grisebach pointed out the reflective nature of the dialectical method in general and showed that thinking in paradoxes, too, deceives man in regard to the nature of the real and leads him away from the actual experience of a real transcendent (his fellowman). For by the rational comprehension of the relationship of the I and the Thou, this relationship, no matter how paradoxically it may be conceived, has become an immanent truth, and all real tension and conflict between the I and the Thou has been theoretically overcome. As an immanent truth, this dialectical relationship complies with the principle of identity, and, by the mind's grasping it as a dialectical principle, the actual experience of a real transcendent is no longer possible. Such an experience, however, as it occurs to man by the contradiction of his fellowman, defies all rationalization and constitution and is an essentially contingent experience.[6]

In his book *Der Gott der neuzeitlichen Metaphysik*, in which he attempts to show how the contemporary intellectual situation, especially in Europe, is conditioned by the development of metaphysics from Cusanus to Heidegger, Walter Schulz sees the historical link of modern metaphysics with the metaphysics of the past in the mediating systematic relation (dialectic) between man and God. In the metaphysics of the past, the unity between man and God was stressed; in contemporary metaphysics, their contrast is emphasized. But the common constitutive or theoretical character of the metaphysics of the past and the present becomes obvious when Schulz says: "Gleichwohl ist allen gegensätzlichen Bestimmungen etwas gemeinsam: die Denker der neuzeitlichen Metaphysik denken Gott und Mensch in und durch den gegenseitigen Bezug, sei dieser Bezug nun als Gegensatz oder als Einheit ge-

---

[6] Cf. E. Grisebach, *Gegenwart*, especially chapter IV entitled: "Die Krisis der Erkenntnis". In the paragraph, entitled: "Der letzte Rettungsversuch der Erkenntnis", Grisebach shows the reflective and theoretical nature of the dialectical method with special reference to Kierkegaard. In a long footnote to the 12th chapter, entitled: "Vom Gestern, Heute und Morgen", Grisebach points out that Heidegger's ontology in *Sein und Zeit* represents another cycle of the self and misses the problem of *Gegenwart* (actual experience). The dialectical method as a paradox is also criticized by Grisebach in *Freiheit und Zucht*. In chapter XIX, entitled: "Zwei Vorkämpfer Kirchlicher Theologie" (zu Erich Przywara's S. J. Analogia entis), Grisebach exposes the dialectical *theologoumena* of Przywara and of Barth as immanent systems. In spite of their difference *in principle*, the former representing an *analogia entis* and the latter an *analogia spi–ritus*, they are both revealed by Grisebach as two cycles of the human self, which are constituted from two different underlying premises.

setzt."[7] In Schulz's book, the historical or situational character of the existential approach (Heidegger's metaphysics) becomes very clear, when Schulz sees in Heidegger the philosopher who thinks against metaphysics[8], but who, nevertheless, adopts a fundamental point of this metaphysics in the positive sense, namely, the insight into man's finiteness and temporality. The dialectical relationship between man and the transcendent in Heidegger's thinking is circumcsibed by Schulz as follows: "Die neuzeitliche Metaphysik hat immer wieder gesucht, dem Menschen diese seine Bedingtheit vor Augen zu führen, indem sie ihn von dem Anderen seiner selbst her verstand... An ihm selbst verstehbar, durchwaltet und trägt das Sein das Seienden das Seiende, das vom Sein ontologisch scharf zu unterscheiden ist, und das doch, sofern es seiend ist, auf das Sein als sein dialektisch Anderes verweist.[9]

The existential alternative for coping with the current crisis of truth has thus been revealed as another historical cycle of the human self, or as another methodological self-projection of man in the world from a particular existential situation. It was man's need for new self-determination and his concern about the authenticity of his existence under circumstances where, after the collapse of his old world of culture, he had been stripped naked that moved him to approach being from a different angle. He discarded the world as a starting-point and sought being on the premise of his being-there or on the premise of his existential consciousness, which revealed itself as either a manifestation of being (Heidegger) or nothing (Sartre). By the constitution of an *existential logos* through the dialectical method on an entirely subjective premise, i.e., in effect the constitution of human existence itself as a dialectical principle, it can hardly be claimed, however, that the whole truth has been embraced and that, for this reason, the crisis of truth has been resolved. The existential alternative is nothing but another form of human self-transcendence, which leads man away from his actual experience and, as such, is metaphysical. Just like any other historical philosophical project, it has invited criticism and has caused new philosophical outlooks and alternatives to be developed by way of reaction. In this way, the historical character of existential metaphysics is clearly revealed.

The question now remains as to the character of the dialectical alternative for dealing with the contemporary crisis of truth. Here is

[7] *Der Gott der neuzeitlichen Metaphysik*, p. 112.
[8] In this regard, cf. F. H. Heinemann, *Existentialism and the Modern Predicament*, chapter VI, entitled: "Heroic Defiance".
[9] *Der Gott der neuzeitlichen Metaphysik*, p. 110.

meant chiefly the Marxian and neo-Marxian alternatives. Is the dialectical alternative as metaphysical as the functionalistic and existential alternatives turned out to be? Is it another cycle of the human self, which, by human self-transcendence, transgresses the empirical limit, i.e., man's actual experience of the real transcendent (i.e., his fellowman, who, by calling him in question, remains man's permanent stumbling block)? And does this philosophical alternative in the end also turn out to be a contingent human vision of truth, which was constituted in the light of particular historical circumstances or a definite existential situation? That this is the case has already been abundantly shown by our discussion of the dialectical alternative. Here we shall merely show briefly the metaphysical character of the dialectical approach to dealing with the crisis of truth. It is its metaphysical nature which makes it another dogmatic system in the history of philosophy. By its insistence on having alone embraced the truth, it, just like the functionalistic and existential projects, leads man into isolation and self-seclusion. He becomes the prisoner of his own self-constituted truth. He is unable to break away from himself and find the way towards the outside, towards his fellowman as the real transcendent. By imagining himself as the executor of the historical law, with which he merges by comprehending it as a materialistic dialectical principle, he becomes the prisoner of his own self-constituted truth and misses his actual experience, namely, the permanent crisis in which he finds himself with his fellowman on account of the controversial nature of their respective truth-perspectives. The experience of the crisis of his own truth, which he shares with his fellowman, would make him realize that not his self-constituted historical logos but the very crisis itself is the true field of his thinking and acting; for it is through the very controversial relationship that holds between himself and his fellowman, or else between their visisons of truth, that man is referred to his fellowman. It follows that only by self-restriction to his actual experience can he be freed from the claims of his own truth and be allowed to live an authentic life, i.e., a life in accordance with his real nature as a historical being, and in accordance with the needs of the particular existential situation in which he happens to find himself. On account of their total character and their claim to universality, however, any of the contemporary philosophical alternatives for dealing with the current crisis of truth deprives man of this authentic experience by demanding absolute conformity to its particular method of trying to master the crisis. Consequently, it demands man's total surrender to its respective doctrine.

The dialectical alternative does this by the constitution of a material historical logos, which fulfils itself by a dialectical movement, thus causing history to assume a lawlike character. This dialectical nature of history allows man to read from it its meaning and purpose. He comprehends this purpose by the dialectical structure of history, and, by so doing, blends with it and hence with the reason of the world. By possessing the historical logos as an immanent truth, man is able to dispose of history and to lead an authentic existence by falling into step with the dialectical movement of the historical logos. It is this constitution of the specific historical epochs by the dialectical movement of the historical logos which enabled Hegel to state: What is reasonable is real and what is real is reasonable; for it is easy to see how, in the dialectical method, truth and reality coincide.

Hegel regards the dialectical movement of the historical logos from the idealist point of view. To him, world history is the externalization of the spirit in the process of its gradual self-emancipation, i.e., returning to itself in absolute purity. "Die Weltgeschichte", says Hegel, "ist die Darstellung des göttlichen, absoluten Prozesses des Geistes in seinen höchsten Gestalten, dieses Stufenganges, wodurch er seine Wahrheit, das Selbstbewusstsein über sich selbst erlangt. Die Gestaltungen dieser Stufen sind die welthistorischen Volksgeister, die Bestimmtheiten ihres sittlichen Lebens, ihrer Verfassung, ihrer Kunst, Religion und Wissenschaft. Diese Stufen zu realisieren, ist der unendliche Trieb des Weltgeistes, sein unwiderstehlicher Drang; denn diese Gliederung sowie ihre Verwirklichung ist sein Begriff."[10] Marx, on the other hand, as well as Lenin and the contemporary Marxian thinker, Herbert Marcuse, regard the historical logos from the materialist point of view. As we have already shown, they conceive the historical logos as manifesting itself in the changing economic conditions, which are the result of the dialectical relationship that holds between man and the world. The changing tools of production condition the changing ways of production, and these, in turn, determine the structural change of society, so that, ultimately, the rift between social structure and way of production is healed. When this happens, man is free, and is one with truth and reality. His consciousness has finally been changed from one that thinks in terms of private and selfish interests to one that thinks in terms of general or social interests.

Thus Marxian dialectic also comprehends history as an immanent truth, with which man must be consciously blended if he wishes to lead

[10] "Der Endzweck" (des Geistes), in: *Hegel*, ed. by F. Heer, p. 97.

an authentic existence. In the Marxian philosophy of history, Hegel's formula: What is reasonable is real and what is real is reasonable, is still valid, except that, now, the economic (material) process determines man's consciousness and thus philosophy, instead of the other way around. But even in Marxian dialectic, it is really philosophy that determines the material process, in as much as Marxian philosophy constitutes the historical logos as an "objective" economic law.[11] We shall here merely quote the fundamental thesis of historical materialism, according to which the dialectical change from one social structure to another takes place by revolution: "Die Produktionsweise des materiellen Lebens bedingt den sozialen, politischen und geistigen Lebensprozess überhaupt. Es ist nicht das Bewusstsein der Menschen, das ihr Sein, sondern umgekehrt ihr gesellschaftliches Sein, das ihr Bewusstsein bestimmt."[12]

By comprehending history as being governed by an economic law and so disposing of it, man disposes of his future as well. He becomes the master of his own destiny, and, in this sense, and earth-bound god. By disposing of history as an immanent truth, he is able to "solve" all problems and to overcome all conflicts and contradictions and, finally, to bring about the Golden Age, thus making true man's perpetual dream. But the question is whether man can accomplish this in reality or only in theory and therefore in his imagination? Marxism turns out to be the resuscitation of metaphysics by the constitution of a universal truth, namely, the conception of a historical logos based on a historical premise. In the functionalistic alternative, it was the mysterious functional power of language through which man could fuse with the world; in the existential alternative, it was the puzzle of man's being-there that revealed the absolute as incomprehensible to him, something which he could not reach with his mind because he was himself imbedded in it and encompassed by it; in the dialectical alternative, it was man's productive power which, miraculously, blended man with the law of history and, in this way, with the world.

In regard to the conception of such a historical logos, we must again refer to Eberhard Grisebach, who, in his *Was ist Wahrheit in Wirklichkeit?* and *Die Schicksalsfrage des Abendlandes*, has shown the dangers of the conception of a historical logos of any kind as a necessary universal truth. He has pointed out that this amounts to another self-estrangement of man from reality, i.e., from man's actual contingent experience

[11] The classical formulation by Marx of the principal theses of *historical materialism* are found in the foreword of *Critique of the Political Economy*.
[12] Quoted from *Grundlagen der marxistischen Philosophie*, p. 347.

of the real transcendent (the contradiction of his fellowman), and that this act of human self-transcendence converts our human truths into lies. It is to the dogmatic and fanatical character of our constituted truths and the consequent total clash of these truths that Grisebach ascribes the downfall of western culture and the catastrophe that had befallen the west (both mentioned works of Grisebach's were written during the Second World War). In *Was ist Wahrheit in Wirklichkeit*, Grisebach exposes the purely academic character of the dialectical method of whatever kind, methods by which their adherents tried to acknowledge the problems and conflicts of our time as real, but at the same time rendered them harmless by dialectical construction and by the rational conception of the contradictory relation as a dialectical principle. By this arbitrary procedure of subsuming the opposites under a dialectical law, reality became constituted as a rational whole, and actual contradiction as well as contingent experience as depending on it were theoretically overcome. Grisebach says: "Es handelte sich um eine durchaus akademische Problematik, die als schwacher Widerschein einer europäischen Revolution die Geister beschäftigte. Es nistete sich ein Zweifel an aller Systematik und Dogmatik ein. Problematik und Dialektik wurden zur grossen Mode... Eine historisch gebildete Generation bot fertige Lösungen des Problems in Fülle an. Man wusste ja längst aus der Geschichte, dass Revolutionen und Reaktionen abwechselten, dass alles in einer Dialektik sich entwickelt hatte, so hatten Schelling und Hegel einst gelehrt. Man bekannte sich deshalb ruhig zu einer Problematik, gab die starren Grundsätze wissenschaftlicher Erkenntnis auf. Aber für die eigene wahre dialektische Geschichtsphilosophie liess man den Widerspruch und die Krise durchaus nicht gelten."[13]

With this Grisebach has hit the nail on the head. The dogmatic character of the dialectical alternative, its insistence that history moves by an objective law (which is conceived by the historian from a definite assumed premise and, in this sense, is subjective), makes its advocates blind to the fact that their alternative is itself in a crisis. It renders them blind to the fact that it is historical itself, in that it has been conceived (as has any other philosophical perspective that has ever been developed throughout human history) in a particular historical situation, and, in its turn, will change the situation, i.e., invite the criticism and contradiction of other philosophical visions and approaches, which may be more in line with the new situation that has developed. In other words, the dialectical approach to dealing with the present crisis of

---

[13] *Was ist Wahrheit in Wirklichkeit*, pp. 11–12.

truth constitutes history only theoretically, but remains itself subject to our actual historical experience, namely, the permanent crisis in which our various historical projects find themselves as a result of the continual controversy over the question of truth between man and his fellowman. "Zukunft," says Grisebach, "wird uns in unserer kritischen Lage, als Wirklichkeit, durch Begrenzung und notwendige Auseinandersetzung hinreichend gegeben. Es besteht kein Grund, in der gegenwärtigen Krise zu verzweifeln. Der Seinsmodus unserer künftigen Wirklichkeit als echter Gemeinschaft wird einmal unsere Verantwortlichkeit heissen. Sie schliesst die Anerkennung der gegenwärtigen Krise des Wahrheitsbegriffs ein und lehrt uns, was Wahrheit in Wirklichkeit ist."[14]

From this it follows that the real ground of the world cannot be theoretically conceived, no matter from what premise such rational conception takes place; and that holds true for all philosophical projects or perspectives that have ever been developed. The real ground of the world cannot be theoretically conceived or rationally constituted because it is the very ground that calls in question our theoretically conceived truths. It is the experience of the permanent crisis of our truths as a result of the opposition or contradiction of the other. This is clearly shown by the controversial relation in which the historical philosophical projects stand with each other and are referred to each other. We mentioned examples thereof in our discussion of the anthropological character of philosophical systems, and, obviously, this is also true in the case of the three contemporary philosophical alternatives for dealing with the present crisis of truth. The history of philosophy has clearly shown that the crisis of our truth itself is the *sufficient reason* of our truth, and that the actual experience of this crisis (which we share with our fellowmen) clearly outlines the empirical limit of our truth and our knowledge. If this were realized by the subscribers to the various philosophical visions of truth, a real encounter, real coexistence and real peace would become possible between man and his fellowman and between nation and nation. Then the total clash between different human visions of truth which, we observed, was the result of absolute self-transcendence, would be avoided.

The controversial relation that obtains as the real ground and as the sufficient reason among the various philosophical systems and projects, as they have been advanced throughout the history of philosophy up to the present day, causes the truth of man's non-comprehen-

14 *Was ist Wahrheit in Wirklichkeit*, p. 42.

sion of *the* Truth to dawn as a *docta ignorantia*. The empirical limit of our truth, which is experienced in the controversy with the other, makes us become acutely aware of the *real* transcendence of the absolute and of the fact that we are unable to reach or comprehend it by systematic or methodological constitution of any kind, positive or negative. Such theoretical conception is nothing but a myth, and a dangerous one at that. In the sense now that in the controversial relation that holds between historical philosophical systems the truth of the *real* transcendence of the absolute dawns, this controversial relation possesses a metaphysical horizon. We may also say that truth and reality are merged in this very relation.

In metaphysical respect, then, the history of philosophy teaches us the lesson that the absolute is *really* transcendent, and that, because of this, the philosopher cannot make any statements about the nature of the absolute at all, for he cannot possibly "know" whether or not it exists. Therefore the lesson we learn from the history of philosophy is that the empirical limit of our truth and our knowledge, as it was outlined by the controversial relation that holds among the historical philosophical truths, refers philosophy to the field of critical experience. As a critical empirical science, it finds itself under an obligation to observe the truth of the *real* transcendencce of the absolute. This *real* transcendence of the absolute is experienced by man in the crisis-situation in which the philosophical projects that were conceived throughout human history invariably found themselves.

In conclusion it may be said that, on the grounds of the permanent crisis in which the historical philosophical projects find themselves with one another, the history of philosophy reveals philosophy as being restricted to the field of becoming. It could thus be defined as the *science of actuality* because of the contingent nature of its various perspectives of truth, which are posited by man and his fellowman in controversy under particular existential circumstances, and which, invariably, call each other in question. The history of philosophy, therefore, teaches us that truth is always both systematic as well as historical. Philosophy, as the science of actuality, constitutes reality in the form of ever new perspectives of truth in conformity with the changing circumstances of life. It may thus be stated that in the historical nature of philosophy theory and practice, truth and reality, reason and experience merge. Through this historical nature, being presents itself as becoming and all necessity shows itself as contingency. By its various philosophical systems and methods, the history of philosophy writes the story of human existence.

D. *The Ethics of the History of Philosophy*

From the ethical point of view, the history of philosophy teaches us that the controversial relation among philosophical systems or projects, or else the crisis-situation in which all human truths and concepts, scientific, historical, philosophical or theological, constantly find themselves, is of moral significance as well. It teaches us that man's *ethical existence* cannot possibly be realized by deduction from a rationally constituted ethical principle or a rationally conceived ethics of whatever kind, whether conceptual or analytical. For such a theoretical conception of ethical truths is at once being called in question by the conception of another one from a different point of view. The theoretical and controversial character of ethical truth can briefly be shown by the answers that have been developed in reply to the fundamental question about the basic criteria or the foundation of the good act. The rationalists answer that the good act should be based on or should have its sufficient reason in the self-evident moral principles in the mind (Descartes). The empiricists say that the touch-stone of good and evil is the pleasure and pain principle (Locke). The transcendalists and the idealists reply that the good act should be founded on duty as a formalization of the will by reason (Kant, Fichte, Hegel, Rickert). The pragmatists argue that the moral act should be measured in terms of utility and efficaciousness (F.C.S. Schiller, W. James, J. Dewey). But, cry the existentialists, the only reality is man in his being-there, hence the moral act must be based on man's decision as to what he really is, a being-to-death, a failure, a being-to-nothing (Heidegger, Jaspers, Sartre). This is nonsense, reply the positivistic functionalists, good and evil and the moral act can only be analyzed and described in accordance with the rules of the respective language game that deals with moral talk, or else the moral act can be inferred only from the knowledge of the particular circumstances under which man acts, and whether his action complies with certain conventional values in order to merit the term good, which, in this way, becomes a second order concept (Wittgenstein, Ryle, Austin). The moral act, insist the Marxians, is a free act, in the sense that man acts in such a way that his immediate material interest falls together with the interest of the whole. If this happens, then man blends with the historical logos, i.e., the inevitable emergence of a free classless society, by which process man's mind or consciousness also undergoes a process of change; from an individual consciousness with private interests, it develops into a social consciousness with general interests.

From this brief historical sketch of ethical truth, the conclusion can be drawn that a theoretically conceived ethics may have a relative and limited validity only, in that it is developed on the basis of the prevalent problems of a particular period. Thus the ethical views of the contemporary alternatives for coping with the present crisis of truth result from the very nature of the crisis. As these various visions of truth were all developed in consequence of the collapse of the old culture that was based on classical metaphysics (i.e., the conceptual construction of an absolute), it is not surprising that they are all anti-metaphysical in character. It may be said that any metaphysics in the classical sense of the word is outlawed by them as immoral because it misguides man and deprives him of the possibility of leading an authentic and therefore an ethical existence. Metaphysics in the classical sense of the word renders man unfree.

It is for this reason that the functionalistic project of truth insists upon the therapeutic method, i.e., curing philosophy from the pathology of metaphysics and so trying to convert it from a theory about the world into a practice of clarifying the functions of language in describing the world. In this way, ethics, too, becomes descriptive. By subjecting it to the functionalistic method, it loses its subjective character and becomes "objective" or "neutral". Only after having been "cured" by the therapeutic method, therefore, can man be said to live an authentic existence, in the sense that he is now free from all metaphysical pathology and can act reasonably, i.e., either in accordance with scientific statements or in conformity with the common sense of ordinary language. The specific historical character of the functionalistic method issues from man's disappointment with traditional culture and from his desire to conform with the unheard of progress of the sciences and technology, which alone seem to be able to gratify all his needs. In the chapter dealing with the functionalistic alternative for coping with the crisis of truth, we have already shown that this philosophical project is one definite methodological constitution of the world among others, which has been conceived under particular circumstances and is, for this reason, historical and cannot avoid subjectivity. If this is the case, the ethics of the functionalistic vision of truth can be described as neutral only within the precincts of its method, i.e., if the underlying premises and assumptions of this method are accepted, but not outside it. That this is so, is shown by the controversial nature of the functionalistic method, e.g., the questionable nature of its premises and assumptions, which were so clearly revealed by Ernest Gellner and so severely criticized by Marcuse.

The existential alternative outlaws classical metaphysics by showing that, by the constitution of the absolute from the world, no absolute is really won because of the finite character of the constitutive act as such, and because man cannot step outside this act. According to the existential approach, classical metaphysics is immoral because it estranges man from himself and causes his existence to become unauthentic. An authentic existence can only be arrived at, if the moral act is based on man's decision to be himself, i.e., by man's heroic act of living up to his historicity, temporality, periodicity and finiteness. It is through this act that man comes to understand himself as the manifestation of being or else as being condemned to freedom. But in this respect, it is the outspoken subjective character of ethical truth that renders it controversial. For it is based on the methodological constitution of human existence as standing in a dialectical relationship with being or else with the nothing. In other words, in the existential vision of truth, morality is based on the existential principle as a dialectical principle, whereby the metaphysical manifests itself in man's specific need of reviewing the nature of his authentic existence after the collapse of the old values, especially after the First and Second World Wars.

The dialectical Marxian perspective of truth rejects all classical metaphysics as immoral because it sees in it the ideological superstructure of the exploiting class. The moral act becomes possible only if the gulf between theory (philosophy) and practice (the real historical situation, i.e., the real needs of proletarian man) is bridged. That is to say, the moral act becomes possible when philosophy becomes one with economics and politics and takes the part of the proletarian class as the productive class. The moral act is so identified with the productive act as an act of freedom, i.e., the leading by man of an authentic existence presupposes that the means of production are in the hands of the immediate producers. It is the constitution of the productive act as the dialectical law of history (which turns man into an economic being governed by basic material needs) that reveals the specific historical position of the dialectical alternative. The conception of the productive act as the dialectical law of history has its roots in the class struggle, which set in in the course of the 19th century as a result of the rapid industrialization of western and central Europe. It is the Marxian interpretation of the productive act and the productive forces in general as the dialectical law of history that gives the dialectical alternative a metaphysical flavour and which renders it controversial.

If the contemporary philosophical alternatives for coping with the current crisis of truth are all methodological attempts at rearranging the world and reassessing the meaning of human existence in a specific historical situation, i.e., in view of the collapse of the old world of culture, they are perspectives of truth that are referred to one another by their very controversial nature. The controversial relation that exists among them calls in question their theoretically conceived ethical truths and principles as well. The fact that these ethical truths find themselves in a crisis shows that the *ethical ground* cannot be a theoretical conception, but, just like the *real ground* of the human logoi, is precisely that which calls in question all theoretical ethics. The ethical ground of all our truth-perspectives, therefore, is the very crisis itself, by which they are referred to one another and which is actually experienced by all men. The real moral act, therefore, rests on an empirical foundation in the true sense of the word. It applies to all men and not only to a definite group subscribing to one particular perspective of truth. The real moral act cannot be derived from a theoretically conceived ethical principle of whatever kind, because such a theoretically deduced act is invariably controversial and thus points beyond itself, to its own negation. The real moral act, however, hails from the daily dealings between myself and my fellowman. It takes its origin in the controversy and conflict in which I find myself with the members of my family, my friends, my professional colleagues, etc. It issues from the common experience of the crisis by man and his fellowman as a result of the controversial relation that holds between their truths, whether these truths are of a personal, a scientific, a philosophical or an ideological kind. It is on the grounds of the actual crisis, therefore, that all men are referred to each other. The history of philosophy teaches us that the real moral act is historical in the sense that the process of culture and civilization in reality depends upon the cooperation between man and his fellowman on the field of the crisis, which they share in common, in the spirit of mutual good will and understanding. It is true that, by imagining himself to be in possession of *the* truth, man again and again puts himself as absolute, thus bringing about a head-on collision with his fellowman, which often results in a catastrophe, but after having bumped his head, he is always flung back onto the field of his actual experience. In spite of our proneness to self-transcendence, we do act with self-restraint and with due consideration for our fellowman, if we really want to keep things going. A good example is marriage, where two different people must do all in their power to make the best out of the situation in which they find themselves and to turn the crisis, which they share in common, into the very ground of close cooperation and affiliation, if the marriage is to be a success. If they fail to do that and cannot, by mutual tolerance, good will and understanding, take the sting out of their inevitable differences and conflicts, the marriage is bound to break up. In other words, the controversial relation among individual human beings, or else their outlook on life, their vision of truth, whether of a private or professional nature, but also the relation among various ideological, cultural and national groups, are always actual historical relations, which shed light upon the particular nature of an individual historical truth (i.e., under which particular historical circumstances it has been conceived) and by which individuals or groups of individuals are referred to one another.

In this way, the *empirical limit* that is outlined by the controversial relation obtaining between two human logoi is also shown to be an *ethical ought;* for this controversial relation is actually experienced as the mutual limitation of man's and his fellowman's ego. It should be remembered that human truths are at the same time self-projections of man in a particular existential situation. It is thus obvious that the crisis, being the result of the controversial relation of human truths by which they are bound together, is not only the logical, empirical and ontological ground of human truth, but is also its *ethical ground*. In short, in the crisis, or else the controversial relation that holds between two human logoi, truth and reality are merged, so that authentic and thus ethical existence is possible only, if man and his fellowman confine themselves to the crisis as the *sufficient reason* of human truth and the *real ground* of human existence. For by the controversial relation that holds between the human logoi or visisons of truth, man and his fellowman are actually referred and restricted to the field of contingent becoming as the field of experiential reality. As an *ethical ought*, the empirical limit invites man to exercise self-control and to restrict himself to the field of historicity and actual becoming as a presupposition for any kind of positive and fruitful cultural activity in real communication, coexistence, cooperation and peace with the other. It may also be said that this *ethical ought*, as it hails from our actual experience, admonishes man to observe his *empirical limit* or that it makes him become conscious of his limitations and the fact that he lives not in oneness but in twoness, i.e., in constant reference to his fellowman. The ethical ought, so to speak, warns man not to transgress his empirical limit by the theoretical act of self-transcendence, lest he obstruct his way to *real* transcendence, i.e., to the other as the one that keeps opposing and questioning him and over whom he fails to gain functional control by methodological constitution. If man, however, ignores his actual experience and transcends his empirical limit by positing his own vision of truth as absolute (which he often enough does), he blocks for himself the way to a real ethical existence, i.e., an existence in reference to the other. That is to say, in that case he isolates himself and secludes himself in his own truth or cycle of the self, thereby making a real encounter, real communication, real coexistence with his fellowman impossible. For a real encounter between man and his fellowman can take place only in the field of their actual experience, i.e., the field of the crisis, because only by the experience of the common crisis of their truth-visions are they actually referred to one another and is their respective cycle of the self broken through. Only by this experience are they referred from theory to practice, namely, the eminently practical nature of the moral act. The empirical ethical ought, so to speak, warns us, lest, by putting ourselves as absolute, we estrange ourselves from our nature and move away from reality, having no regard for the other man's truth and adopting an attitude of self-righteousness, intolerance and dogmatism. Such an attitude in self-estrangement could never breed good will and peace, but will, on the contrary, cause quarrelling, disunity and war.[15]

But whatever man does, in whatever way he acts, whether he is conscious of it or not, his thinking and acting occur in terms of the other. He is in constant exchange with him, and this exchange is necessary for his activity, material, intellectual and spiritual. In whatever way he may put himself as absolute, always he is taken to task by

---

[15] In this regard, it is interesting to note how Eberhard Grisebach, in his book *Gegenwart*, especially in the chapter on "Satanism", pp. 467–472, seeks to show the evil and malicious character of academic truth on account of its inevitably egoistical and totalitarian or dogmatic character. We cannot agree that our rationally conceived truths are ipso facto evil. They may be posited in such a way that we remain conscious of their historical nature. They may of course become evil if posited in an absolute manner. However, as historical visions of truth, our methodological self-projections into the world are at the same time views of reality, which we cannot help developing. In the light of the total crisis and the total clash of human truths as experienced by Grisebach in his time, it becomes nevertheless understandable that Grisebach attempts to show that the old acknowledged virtues: wisdom, fortitude, righteousness, justice, etc., as well as those gifts that were regarded as constituting the greatness of the human spirit, e.g., originality, autonomy, good will, spirit of enterprise, clear reasoning, lead into isolation and to self-seclusion, for they have their origin in the human self. Their egoistical character reveals them as vices, for, as the unfolding of the human self, they block the way to the other and make real community with him impossible. As now these virtues can be interpreted and conceived in different ways, from differently conceived underlying moral principles or "real grounds", a clash of the different cycles of the self or the will is inevitable.

the other. Only, if he puts himself absolute, there is no creative and fruitful controversy in the spirit of friendship and good will (as there would be if he acted with self-control or self-restraint), but there is a total clash between him and his fellowman, between his own truth and that of the other, who is then compelled to assert himself against the total claim of his opponent, or who may even posit his own truth in as absolute a manner against that of his adversary. In a situation where two truths confront each other in a total manner, the clash and the crisis are as total. In this case, the fruitful controversy of the natural crisis deteriorates into a bad quarrel, constructive cooperation in controversy becomes destructive force against force, good will turns into hostility, genuine community and real communication are broken down and existence in twoness changes into existence in oneness, i.e., an existence in isolation, frustration and despair. Is this not an adequate picture of our world to-day, where indeed such a total clash of the contemporary visions of truth takes place, where ideology stands against ideology and where war and revolution in their cold and hot form have become a permanent phenomenon?

The lesson we learn from this is that the attempt to overcome the crisis of truth is something that is natural, in the sense that it points to man's true nature as being controversial and historical. Its actual experience by all men as the empirical limit of their truth and their knowledge marks it as man's common field of action, as the very ground of all human culture and civilization. It is this that turns the crisis into the moral reason for human truth. If the crisis of our truth were seen as the true ethical ground, the problem of ethics would no longer exist. Then the question why there is not the same progress in man's moral behaviour as there is in the sciences and in technology loses its meaning. This arose from the spurious idea that man's moral act could be won from reflection, i.e., the theoretical conception of ethical truth. This, however, has been shown to be impossible because of the controversial nature of every such conception. If, however, man's moral act hails from the controversy in which he is inevitably involved with his fellowman in constituting the world in the sciences and the humanities and is thus shown to be absolutely practical and not theoretical at all, there can be no talk about man being morally retarded. Man would always act morally if he acted under the impression and in full awareness of the inevitably critical and controversial nature of his truth, no matter what stage of perfection his methodological skill had reached in formulating his truth systematically. What the history of philosophy teaches us most convincingly is that there is no such thing as moral progress, but that there are only historical conceptions of moral truth, which are developed under specific existential circumstances, and which are always controversial and in a state of crisis. The actual experience of this crisis points to the controversial relation as the practical ground of all moral conduct, which is present everywhere where human beings or groups of human beings (cultural, ideological, political groups) enter into contact and communication with one another. In other words, we become aware that in all our acts, practical or theoretical, in the private sphere of family life and of friendship, in the more public fields of the sciences, technology and the arts, the moral ought is implied to heed the empirical limit as it is delineated by our fellowman's message and address to us, by his claim to be heard.

The positive acceptance of the crisis by man and his fellowman means at the same time the acceptance of the other's contradiction. In accepting this contradiction, I keep my mind open to the other and, in so doing, I gain understanding of the particular existential situation in which he finds himself, i.e., of the particular needs, interests and aspirations, which cause him to posit his truth in opposition to mine. In accepting his contradiction and keeping myself open for his claims, I become aware of the message he conveys to me by the postulation of his own truth. This message urges me to listen to him, it challenges me to exercise self-restraint in my response and in my dealings with him and to be gentle, modest and humble in my approach to him. It may also be said that he urges me to act responsibly in the sense of responding to him in this manner. If I do and take up his message in a responsible way, I then enter into real communication and establish a real community with him, which leads to peaceful coexistence and creative cooperation in the field of our common actual experience and creative activity. If, by my own free choice, I am *willing* to open my mind to him, I begin to achieve a break-through out of the cylce of my own truth and my own will. By this free decision to restrict myself to the field of my actual experience of the crisis, I have subordinated my will to my reason in that I act reasonably, i.e., in accordance with my true nature as a controversial being. By acting reasonably in the previous sense, I simultaneously act morally, for, in so doing, I am in step with reality, i.e., the experience of the crisis as the *sufficient reason* and *real ground* of human truth and existence. I may now be said to lead an *authentic* as well as an *ethical existence*, i.e., an existence free from the claims of my own truth. For by the reasonable act of self-restraint to the field of the actual experience which I share with my fellowman, I turn from myself to the other, from the immanent to the emanent. In being aware of the actual experience of the *real* transcendent (my fellowman), I now come to lead an existence with reference to the other, whom I encounter with respect, tolerance, understanding and good will. The moral act, which is inextricably interwoven with this authentic or ethical existence, may thus be said to consist in always acting with reference and with regard to the other, no matter under what historical and existential circumstances. That means I always act by taking into consideration the special views, needs and interests of the other. By a benevolent exchange of our ideas and views on the ground of the inevitable crisis of our visions of truth, we may be able to cause these ideas to become operative for the benefit of the whole community of men, depending upon the specific conditions under which these ideas and views are put forward.

From this it can be established that the ethics of the history of philosophy is outlined by the controversial relation by which the various historical philosophical systems are linked up with one other. As self-projections of man in a particular historical situation, they reflect man's historical and finite nature. The permanent crisis in which these philosophical projections find themselves reflects man's permanent existential crisis. Although man cannot overcome this crisis, he can deal with it effectively by close cooperation with his fellowman in the very field of the crisis by which they are referred to each other in mutual self-control. The empirical limit of man, which is so clearly outlined by the controversial relation that obtains among the historical philosophical systems, reveals the crisis of our truths as the ethical ground and the moral act as of an outspoken practical nature, which is implied by all our dealings with our fellowmen, whether these dealings are of a practical or theoretical nature. The history of philosophy teaches us thus the futility of man's repeated attempt to derive the authenticity and ethics of human existence from theoretical conception of any kind whatever. Marking off man's empirical limit most clearly, indeed, the history of philosophy teaches man to abandon his attitude of *hubris* with regard to his outlook on life, the world and himself and to substitute this attitude by one of *modesty* and *humility*. This lesson is particularly relevant to the representatives of the various contemporary philosophical perspectives that deal with the present crisis of truth. It would appear as though the moral obligation implied by the history of philosophy to acknowledge the empirical limit of their respective vision of truth and to meet each other on the ground of the very crisis is ignored by the advocates of the various contemporary philosophical projects. They remain ensconced in their own truth, imagining that they have mastered the crisis. They are thus dogmatic, intolerant and aggressive. Small wonder that the world to-day is dominated by *hubris* instead of by *modesty* and *humility*.

THE EXISTENTIAL CHARACTER OF PHILOSOPHY
AND THE PROBLEM OF AUTHENTIC EXISTENCE

From the historical character of philosophy in the above sense, the existential nature of philosophy clearly outlines itself. This existential aspect must not be confused with the existentialism of the existential alternative for coping with the crisis of truth, as we have previously discussed it. It is not based on the methodological constitution of the phenomenon of human existence or on the theoretical conception of the dialectical relation of this phenomenon with the transcendent. But the existential nature of philosophy is actually experienced in the permanent crisis of human truth in general and thus of philosophy as the discipline which seeks to formulate this truth in a general manner.

If we found that the crisis of all human truth is the sufficient reason for all philosophizing and that the actual experience of this crisis by man and his fellowman is the very motor of all human thinking and cultural activity on man's part, it is evident that no theoretically conceived human truth can claim to have overcome the crisis and to have solved all of man's existential problems. As it became obvious from our discussion of the three contemporary alternatives for coping with the crisis of truth, none of them has succeeded in overcoming this crisis. On the contrary, because of the claim to absoluteness and totality of each of these philosophical alternatives, the crisis has been stretched to breaking-point.

From this we learn that the existential character of philosophy cannot be theoretically conceived or constituted at all, but is actually experienced by the philosopher through the crisis in which his self-constituted truth finds itself on account of its being called in question by some other philosopher, or else by the philosophical project of some other thinker, who proposes to deal with the crisis from his specific situation, thus developing his particular vision of truth. In so doing, however, such a thinker raises new problems in his turn and thereby creates a new existential situation, which other thinkers seek to master by the development of new philosophical alternatives, etc..

The existential character of philosophy must thus be traced to man's basic need for coping with certain fundamental problems, as they present themselves in a certain situation, and for overcoming the crisis by the possible solution of those problems. That is why we stated before that philosophy is man's mirror and that each philosophical project or truth-alternative reflects the problems of a specific historical epoch. But since any such proposed alternative for dealing with the problems of a specific historical situation is ipso facto questionable, thus creating new problems and conflicts, the existential character of philosophy in general must be traced to the finite and contingent nature of all human truth. For it is the hard and basic fact of man's finiteness and contingency that renders man's thinking perspectivistic, in the sense that he develops ever new aspects of truth, both about nature and about himself. Man's thinking, therefore, is always action in a specific existential situation, and although this is true for the sciences and for history as well, it becomes particularly evident in philosophy. If, however, the postulation of a philosophical alternative for coping with the crisis of truth is recognized as an existential act on man's part, i.e., an arranging of his surroundings in a rational manner so as to control them and to give his life meaning and purpose, the existential character of philosophy becomes very clear indeed. Such an act is more than a mere theoretical or methodological constitution of the world and of human existence. It always means man's self-realization in the particular situation in which he finds himself. In this respect, no philosophical project is an exception, and the contemporary alternatives for coping with the crisis of truth are, as we have witnessed, desperate attempts on man's part to realize himself by trying to find meaning and purpose in a completely new existential situation, which is marked by the token of totality. What is new about this situation is that the truth-visions that have been developed and that are facing one another to-day are backed by a total technology. In their mutual attempt to destroy one another and to gain sole control of the world, they are able to make use of deadly weapons which threaten to bring about man's complete extinction. In other words, the danger is that the conflict between two total ideologies, that of the East and that of the West, will lead to man's self-destruction by the application of a technology which has itself become total. We have already pointed to the totality of functionalistic thinking, which found expression not only in the functionalistic alternative for coping with the crisis of truth, but also in the dialectical alternative, and to which kind of thinking the existential alternative formed a re-action to the other extreme.

Nothing, however, proves better the existential nature of human thinking in general and of philosophy in particular than this deadly danger which is hovering over man. It shows that the postulation of any human truth, no matter how absolute it is held to be, is, after all, a finite and contingent act, but that such an act assumes a virulent and malignant character if its empirical limits are ignored. The situation in which man finds himself to-day is his need to find a way out of this dilemma; and what better way is there than acknowledging and ac-cepting the existential character of all human thinking in the above sense? If this were to happen and man were to abandon all claim to absoluteness and totality and were to accept the crisis of human truth as inevitable and natural and as the very ground of all human activity and communication, he would not only remove the danger of self-destruction, but would possibly arrive at a more congenial world-view and way of life. Nothing reveals more the existential character of phi-losophy than the acuteness of the contemporary crisis of truth. This experience forces philosophy to take stock of itself and, in critical self-reflection, to reconsider its position, its function and its purpose. As man's tool for self-realization in a particular existential situation, it can never hope to embrace *the* truth, and it should boldly acknow-ledge this fact, thereby acknowledging its own limitation. But in doing so, philosophy performs a constructive task. From a self-constituted world of theory, it leads man to the field of his actual experience, which he shares with his fellowman, namely, the crisis of all human truth. In teaching him to operate from this basis, instead of from his own self-constituted truth, it shows him the way to his fellowman and refers him to the other as his companion in the quest for truth and the nature of human existence. Never has the existential nature of philosophy been so obvious as in man's present existential situation, where the shadow of self-extinction hovers over his life. And for this very reason the task of philosophy has never been so important and so colossal as now that man's very existence is at stake. This task consists in the adoption of a critical and self-critical attitude and, by the acknowledgement of its own limitation and questionable nature, in inducing man to accept his limitation by his fellowman as a positive and not as a negative oc-currence, as something that affirms him as an individual in his own right and yet refers him to his fellowman in the adventure of life. In short, it is the permanent crisis of truth, which is experienced in common by man and his fellowman, that renders philosophy existential and that makes man realize that he lives not in oneness but in twoness. This existential nature of philosophy makes it impossible for man to isolate himself by insisting upon the exclusive rightness and validity of his own truth. Where such total self-righteousness is indulged in, as is the case with the contemporary philosophical alternatives, reality reasserts itself in as absolute a manner, namely, by jeopardizing man's very existence.

From the existential character of philosophy in the above sense, we learn the lesson that all human truth is finite, contingent and questionable. It teaches us man's incapability of knowing *the* truth; for man's question about *the* truth is a permanent one and is asked again and again as the situation changes. In fact, it is the way this question is answered, in accordance with the prevailing problems at a certain historical stage, which determines the new situation.

This brings us to the problem of man's authentic existence, which is closely related to the existential nature of philosophy. If philosophy is man's mirror and finds itself in a permanent crisis and remains problematic, it follows that human existence is an existence in a permanent crisis and is always problematic as well. For we have recognized philosophical projects as suggestions for coping with the crisis of truth in such a way that this crsis is overcome in a rational manner, and truth is found. In short, the problem of man's authentic existence is closely related to the problem of truth. It stands to reason that, if we knew *the* truth, we should also know man's authentic nature, and the problem of man's authentic existence would be solved. The problem of authentic existence may be regarded as fundamental, in is much as it arises from man's basic need to project himself into the world in such a way that he fills it with purpose and with meaning,, thus getting to know himself and his own nature, or, rather, deriving it from his self-conceived structure of the world. In this way, authentic existence may be defined as an existence in line with reality, i.e., reality as it is conceived by the rational or methodological constitution of the world by man. Such methodological constitution of the world remains controversial, however, because it always occurs from a particular historical or existential situation and is only one perspective of truth. From this it follows that the authentic nature of man's existence remains a problem, as it means something else for every philosopher, depending upon the method or approach he applies in organizing reality in a rational manner and upon the premise from which he starts thereby. The idealist, for instance, regards the idea, the concept or the mind as the ground of reality.[1] The materialist, on the other hand, sees matter as the real foundation of the world. To him, mind is only the result of physical functions (the functions of the brain, for example) or more complex or more highly developed matter. Again, it depends on the underlying premise from which the materialist starts, whether he subscribes to a mechanistic, evolutionist or historical kind of materialism.[2] If, now, by man's authentic existence is meant an existence in line with reality, it follows that authentic existence means something else for the idealist than it does for the materialist. For the former, it means to subordinate my material aims and desires to the idea, to reason or mind as the *real ground* of the world. For the latter, it means to be in line with sense-experience, with my desire for pleasure, happiness and usefulness and with the material or economic conditions as they are dictated by my material needs in order to be free from want, hunger, suffering, economic exploitation and political oppression. In short, the question of the authentic nature of man's existence is answered only within the precincts of a certain method that is developed under particular historical circumstances or in a specific existential situation. It is thus answered in different ways and remains problematic. This difference implies a difference in moral standard, since the moral act is derived from man's authentic nature. And only if he acts in conformity with his authentic nature, as it is derived from man's respective vision of the world, does he act morally. And only if this happens, is he free from all conflicts; for then he is in step with reality, as it has been conceived by a certain thinker.

It appears as though the question of man's authentic existence is answered in accordance with the idea or the *model* the respective thinker forms himself of man in conformity with his vision of the world or his vision of truth. Many such models of man have been constructed by philosophers throughout the centuries. Here are a few examples: We have already seen in our introduction that, for Plato and Aristotle, the universe was rational and harmonious and that man was seen as a *rational being*, in the sense that the rational structure of the universe was reflected in his soul. Authentic existence meant for these two outstanding Greek thinkers to live and act in accordance with one's rational nature because, in so doing, man would be in step with the uni-

---

[1] Examples are Descartes, Berkeley, Hegel.
[2] Respective examples are Lamettrie, Spencer, Marx.

verse. Such reasonable action was at the same time moral action. For Plato, this meant that man must strive for universal truth, so that man would have to subordinate his noble affects and his material appetites to reason. If reason ruled supreme and kept the balance, then man was just. The same applied to society and the state, where the three social classes corresponded to the three parts of the soul. If the *archontes* ruled strictly in conformity with the truth and the other classes bowed to their wisdom in wise self-restraint, harmony and justice would prevail. For Aristotle, man was a *rational animal,* in the sense that he used his reason to control his natural instincts and to practise moderation. It was then that he led an authentic existence. Just as in the universe there was not a too much or a too little, but everything was well balanced, so that it could be defined by rational judgment, man should take the way of the *golden mean* in his action as well. Thus the good state was always the moderate state, no matter whether its form was the monarchy, the aristocracy or the democratic republic.

In the Middle Ages, when historical circumstances had changed and man no longer implicitly trusted his reason, man was seen, in the main, as a *creature of faith.* Truth was no longer found by rational insight into nature as was the case among the Greeks, but had been revealed in the gospel and had to be accepted on faith first before it could be investigated by reason. Thus man's authentic existence was really one in faith, and moral action sprang from faith and the love of God.

In modern times, when the medieval vision of truth had broken down and the scholastic method had exhausted itself, man moved himself into the centre of the universe. On the one hand, he saw himself as *res cogitans* (Descartes), who knew God and the universe by his reason, on the grounds of analytical judgment and who, therefore, led an authentic existence as a reasoning and judging being, knowing moral principles to exist as clear and self-evident ideas in his mind. On the other hand, man saw himself as a *creature of experience,* who could know the world and moral action from his experience. He led an authentic existence as long as he followed the teachings of his experience, also as a member of society. If he did so and subordinated his experience to rational insight, he would eventually achieve greater happiness (Locke).

The German philosopher Kant again saw man as a *creature of moral duty.* That is to say, according to him, man led an authentic existence if he lived up to the autonomy of his reason, by which he could transcend the world of space and time or the world of understanding and penetrate to the *thing-in-itself*. This he found as the *categorical impera-tive* or the moral law of duty in his mind. Because, said Kant, man *can* act rationally, i.e., in such a way that his action could be declared a universal law, he *ought* to do so.

With Hegel, man is seen as the *torch-bearer of the world-spirit*, which unfolds itself in nature and in world history and, by a dialectical move-ment, returns to itself. Man is blended into world history in as much as he is able to conceptualize this movement of the spirit in his mind. He leads an authentic existence if he keeps in step with the spirit and contemplates its final return to itself as a pure rational concept. Man acts morally if he conceives the state as part of the objective spirit and so as an ethical idea. He must blend himself into the state by subordi-nating his will to the reason of the state, which Hegel conceives as the realization of the ethical idea or the spirit of the people having become visible. As the state, which, as the realization of common consciousness, Hegel calls "*Sittlichkeit*" (social morality or moral order) is the manifes-tation of the spirit at a certain historical stage, it follows that, by subor-dinating himself to its reason, man blends himself into world history.

It is thus evident that man's authentic existence is *constituted* or theoretically conceived under the law of identity. Only if man is in step with reality, is he in line with his true nature. Only if he acts in accor-dance with his true nature, does he act morally, only then is he no longer estranged from himself and free from all conflict. In fact, the law of identity is in operation at any theoretical conception of the authentic nature of human existence, and it is always under this law that this problem is solved. But it is solved in theory only, in reality it remains, since these various "solutions" contradict one another. These "solutions" are thus liable to estrange man from reality and to induce him to lead an unauthentic existence.

In this respect, the contemporary alternatives for coping with the crisis of truth are no exception. If, in linguistic philosophy, man becomes just a functional concept and the meaning of the word "man" depends upon the context within it is used and the particular circumstances under which it is applied, it is only consistent if the same applies to moral concepts. If man (as we noticed when discussing the functiona-list approach) is dissolved into functional relations, which are described in terms of analytical propositions, this corresponds to the description of nature's functional relations in terms of mathematical equations. In this one-dimensional way of thinking, man is blended with the world by the analytical or descriptive method, which dissolves everything into functional processes. The functionalistic approach deals with the problem of man's authentic existence by not accepting it as a problem or by regarding it as a pseudo-problem. For by this approach, man ceases to exist as an individual. If, in contemporary existential philosophy (Heidegger, Sartre), man is conceived as a *being-to-death* or a *being-to-nothing*, it is not surprising that, in this case, authentic existence means to take a resolution to be, in the face of nothing. This act of self-creation in the midst of nothing is an act of freedom, in as much as it frees man from an unauthentic existence in the anonymous world of the sciences, the mass, public opinion, etc., and reconciles him with his true standing as having been thrown into the world as a stranger and as a being-to-nothing. And if, in the materialist dialectical alternative, man is regarded as an *economic animal*, which, by productive action, changes his environment in such a way that man's consciousness is thereby changed and reflects the new conditions, history has moved from a class-conscious to a classless society. Only if this historical law has fulfilled itself, is man able to lead an authentic existence. Only if his consciousness is no longer split between his individual and the general interest and if they coincide, is he free from all conflict and self-estrangement. Under these new conditions, he can now fully realize himself and act responsibly, i.e., in the interest of the whole, whereby his own interest, too, is served.

Since, however, the theoretical conception of man's authentic existence in conformity with the specific truth-perspective of a certain thinker remains controversial and problematic, the question arises as to the *real ground* of man's authentic existence. If man's authentic existence remains a problem as long as it is based on a self-constituted real ground, we must enquire into the very ground which renders it a problem. This ground reveals itself as the controversial relation which exists among the human truth-perspectives and the many contradictory views of the authentic nature of man's existence. In other words, it consists in the very questionability of these conceptions, which questionability we experience as the crisis of our truth. The experience of this crisis, which we all share in common and by which all our self-constituted truth is called in question, should prevent us from deriving the authentic nature of our existence from our truth-perspective of the world. If we have defined man's authentic existence as an existence in reality, we must not substitute reality by theory. For if all theory is called in question in reality by our actual experience of the crisis of our truth, authentic existence, if it is to be one in reality, must be based on this actual experience, instead of on theory. If this happens, it is based on practice, namely, the practice of everyday life by which man enters into controversy, debate and discussion with his fellowman in the various fields of life, in the private field of family affairs, in the professional field of his occupation, in the public field of politics, etc. In all these dealings with his fellowman, man should never forget his natural limitations, which grow from his finiteness and inadequacy of understanding the whole. These limitations he experiences everyday in the dealings with the other, who keeps calling him in question. If he wishes to lead an authentic life, he must observe his natural empirical limits, as they are outlined by the contradiction of the other and by his claim to be heard. He must not overstep these limits by absolute self-transcendence, entrenching himself in his own truth, view or vision, so estranging himself from reality and ignoring his true nature. Authentic existence, as an existence in reality, does not mean an existence in oneness, in the seclusion of one's own self-constituted truth or the truth to which one subscribes. Authentic existence, on the contrary, always means an existence in twoness, i.e., an existence with reference to the other. It means the acceptance and acknowledgement of the questionable character of my own truth and my limitation by the other. It means the acceptance of the other as my constant stumbling block, with whom I must work out our common destiny in a common crisis. Authentic existence is no existence in harmony, nor does it operate under the law of identity. On the contrary, authentic existenc is an existence in natural conflict, resulting from the *unequalness* of men, in the sense that they have to posit their truth under particular circumstances and so from a specific existential situation. Authentic existence means freedom from one's own truth, the ability to move from one's immanent truth towards the emanent truth of one's fellowman. It is he who, through his contradiction and criticism, is the real transcendent; it is not some theoretically conceived ground of the world.

Authentic existence, as an existence in reality, is also an existence in truth, namely, the truth of man's inability to comprehend *the* truth. It is the realization of this truth by man that will induce him to accept the truth of his finiteness, of his inadequacy to go it alone and the need for the other in the quest for truth and the continued creation of cultural values and goods of civilization in connection with this quest. The problem of man's authentic existence cannot be solved because any such solution would have to be a theoretical one, which is, however, controversial again. The problem of authentic existence can only be accepted as natural and inevitable, as an experience that challenges man to continue his search for truth. In accepting the problem of authentic existence in a positive way, however, man leads an authentic existence in as much as, in its acceptance, he accepts himself as problematic and controversial, which, if anything, is his true nature. All in all, the leading of an authentic existence requires of man a reversal of his whole manner of thinking. Instead of seeking to constitute universal truth methodologically, he should come to realize that, for him, universal truth lies in the experience of the crisis of truth, which experience he shares with his fellowman. Such insight would induce him to refrain from seeking his salvation in one human truth or ideology. It would open his eyes to the fact that the world is really a multiversum, that the many aspects of truth developed by man are referred to each other by their very controversial nature and that his self is a broken one, not a harmonious one, which faultlessly blends with nature and the whole universe. In leading an authentic existence, his whole outlook on the world, on life and his fellowman would change. In being keenly aware of his controversial and questionable nature, man would stop thinking and acting in terms of utopias and nursing false hopes of a life of perfect peace and harmony, free from all care, conflict and suffering. He would, instead of indulging in deceptive expectations, do all in his power to co-operate with his fellowman to make life as agreeable as possible for all and to cope with the natural crisis-situation in such a way that the best is won from it for everybody. To move closer to each other on the very field of the crisis in mutual self-restraint, recognition of each other's needs, respect, tolerance and good will is the most that can be reached. Only by this modest and realistic approach to life and the other, are the particular interests of all considered and never by the postulation of one truth as *the* truth, when the interests of others are overridden and people are forced to conform. In leading an authentic existence, however, man changes his attitude of *hubris* to one of *modesty*, based on his actual experience. The act of self-restraint on account of this experience is a moral act, which has no longer a theoretical but an eminently practical foundation.

Authentic existence, in the above sense, does thus clearly link up with the existential nature of philosophy. This is not surprising if we consider that philosophy is man's mirror and reflects his true nature. If man's true nature has been recognized as being controversial and problematic, it is small wonder that philosophy displays the same characteristics. Through critical insight into its own nature and function, it will wisely observe its limits and, in wise self-restraint, confine itself to the field of man's actual experience, instead of losing itself in bloodless analytical abstractions, which have very little to do with man's actual experience and with practical life, or in metaphysical leaps to the transcendent or dialectical conceptions of history, which induce man to lead an unauthentic existence and rouse in him expectations which can never be fulfilled. It can thus be seen that, if philosophy complies with man's actual experience of the permanent crisis of truth, it is possible for man to lead an authentic existence. The new approach to life and the change of attitude and of thinking which would be required by this approach would not be unrewarding to man. The mortal danger to man's very existence on this planet, which is caused by total ideologies backed by a total technology, would thereby be removed, and the unauthentic existence, which people lead in total systems, would be exchanged for an authentic one. And than this fact nothing reveals better the existential nature of philosophy and its link with man's authentic existence, which is at the same time ethical existence because it is an existence in reference to the other. Such authentic existence alone recognizes and respects the other as an individual in his own right, i.e., takes into consideration the qualitative distinction that exists between man and his fellowman on account of the controversial relation that obtains between their truth-perspectives. It alone bases the moral act on man's actual experience of the crisis, which he shares in common with his fellowman, so that moral action arises from the very dealings that take place between himself and his fellowman as an act of mutual self-restraint and modesty. Moral action has existential signifance, in as much as it enables man and his fellowman to enter into close communication with each other and into a dialogue concerning their mutual needs and interests as well as the permanent problem of truth. Moral action, like authentic existence, is no theoretical but an eminently practical affair.

CONCLUSION

The discussion of the contemporary philosophical alternatives for coping with the current crisis of truth as well as the investigation of the nature of truth in general have clearly shown that the crisis of human truth cannot be overcome by theoretical conception or methodological constitution of whatever kind because this crisis is natural, i.e., takes its origin in man's very nature as a historical and controversial being. The attempt at overcoming the crisis on the part of any of the contemporary philosophical visions of truth must therefore be dismissed as a shot into the dark. It is from this attempt that their claim to absoluteness and their dogmatic character must be explained. The conception in an absolute manner of whatever kind of logos, the scientific, historical, philosophical or theological kind, can never set man free and make possible for him an authentic or ethical existence, but will, on the contrary, put him in new chains. Such theoretical conception can never heal the crisis, but, on the contrary, only aggravates it, and it is in its aggravated form that we are experiencing it to-day. The new catastrophe into which man appears to be sliding by the totality of the clash between the contemporary perspectives of truth can only be avoided if philosophers, scientists and politicians from all corners of the world act on the injunction of that which they experience in common, namely, the crisis itself. By making it the common ground of their reflections and their constitutions, they might realize the futility of their attempt to overcome it. But in giving up this abortive attempt and by restricting themselves to the field of their common actual experience and accepting it as their common field of action, they may find themselves abundantly rewarded. They may find that the other one was not at all as he was believed to be. They might discover much more that they had in common with the other one than they had believed possible. If philosophers, scientists and politicians drew nearer to each other and acted in accordance with their actual experience instead of in accordance with their abstracted or theoretically conceived experience, East and West might gradually come to understand each other much better than is the case to-day, and, as a result of it, might accept each other, instead of distrusting and suspecting one another as happens to-day. How much prejudice could be avoided by getting to know one another more intimately! How much more effectively could the use of force be dispensed with and peace be preserved than it can by the insistence of certain contemporary philosophers, scientists and politicians upon the exclusive rightness and righteousness of their own truths! How much more effectively could fear be banished from the world and could the burning problems of mankind, such as overpopulation and undernourishment, be dealt with! Only if philosophers, scientists and politicians descend from the ivory towers of their self-constituted truth and enter the field of actual experience and common action, can mankind become happier. As long as science and technology are used in the race for power of two or more opposing camps, as long as our youth is tempted by lofty ideals based on highly illusory conceptions of the function of science and the process of history, there can be no real peace. The absolutization of a scientific or historical logos is fatal. It leads to a fanatical cult of scientific or historical progress, which is bound to mislead young people. They are in any case prone to regard themselves as the undertakers of "backward views and outlooks on life" and of "worn out values", which no longer have any meaning in modern society or the modern way of life and continued adherence to which widens the gap between that which is practised and that which is preached. Young people are always acutely conscious of this gap and seek to bridge it by keeping in step with reality. They always feel themselves to be the torch-bearers of progress and history. And particularly to-day, where the conflicts and contradictions of the established social order and the clash of ideologies and *Weltanschauungen* have become total, young people will not hesitate to change society by force in order to overcome these conflicts and contradictions, which, on account of their totality, have assumed a menacing character and have become unbearable. In order to resolve inner tensions, which have been stretched to breaking-point, the young intelligentsia is ready to resort to violent revolution. But what will happen after the destruction of the established social order? By what order will it be replaced, if any? The young people's faith in the neo-Marxian doctrines of Ernst Bloch and Herbert Marcuse just means the embracing of another theoretically conceived truth-perspective, which is not only extremely utopian, but which is as total and absolute as are the other contemporary philosophical perspectives. Especially from our discussions of Herbert Marcuse, it became clear that his offered alternative for getting out of our present dilemma is really only an interpretation of the Marxian constitution of the historical logos in the face of present social conditions. In other words, together with Marx, Marcuse knows the course of history because he has constituted it himself as a dialectical logos.

There is no solution to be found by way of any theoretically conceived alternative of whatever kind because it is always perspectivistic and controversial, or else it is itself problematic, provoking contradiction to its offered "solution", and so is itself in a state of crisis. If, however, it were realized that sciences, history, philosophy and politics, in their respective stage of development and with regard to their specific historical problems, are the outcome of the crisis in which they constantly find themselves and of the permanent controversy that is carried on between man and his fellowman and therefore are in a constant state of becoming, people would take up a very different attitude towards these disciplines as well as towards their fellowman. They would then not expect of them any miraculous solution or a resolution of the crisis. Instead of gazing fixedly at a promised land or losing themselves in vain in dreams of a Golden Age, a better mankind and a better society, they would then turn to reality and to their fellowman. They would then realize that man will always remain man, that what they call better is so only in terms of their theoretical construction or their imagination. It would dawn upon them that their fellowman is the one with whom they must work together in order to alleviate their suffering and that of their fellowman in the natural crisis and in order to make easier for themselves and for the other the struggle of life. Not only would they realize the completely utopian nature of man's absolute logoi, but they would also see that the overcoming of the natural conflict by any method whatsoever would mean the termination of the creative controversy between man and his fellowman, which is necessary for the gratification of man's vital needs. The overcoming of the natural crisis, the field of man's actual experience, would thus be tantamount to the cessation of all life and hence to the nothing. For as long as man exists, there will be conflict and controversy; and because there is controversy, there will be science, history, philosophy, politics and theology.

It is thus man who, by cooperation with his fellowman, keeps arranging and rearranging the world in the sciences and in the humanities and, in so doing, keeps going the process of culture and civilization as a whole and, in this sense, keeps in progress the process of history. The sciences and the humanities, but also the human science of theology, must thus be seen as so many changing aspects of truth and reality, about which man, in controversy with his fellowman, discovers ever new dimensions. These aspects of truth differ not only in quantity but also in quality. Their qualitative difference lies in the specific field which these various disciplines investigate and the specific methods of investigation which the apply. The method of the natural sciences, for example, as a systematic enquiry into the world of material things, is fundamentally different from the historical method. The indiscriminate application of the scientific method in the humanities leads to a process of levelling, functionalization and quantification. But man, as we have observed, behaves differently from a material thing. He refuses to be subjected to the functionalistic method and keeps calling it in question. This fact alone points to a decisive difference between man and a material thing. The attempt, therefore, by neo-positivistic philosophy to apply the scientific or else the functionalistic method to man, to human action and conduct as well as to human organizations and institutions, such as society, for instance, leads to a quantitative levelling of the natural qualitative differences that exist between man and the world of things. By the reduction of the humanities to the metrical world and the super-cession of the hermeneutic method (as the appropriate method for the humanities) by the functionalistic method, an artificial world of auto-mation is created, into which man is absorbed to the extent of being controlled by it, instead of remaining in control of it.

The various truth-perspectives in the sciences, in the humanities and in theology represent the realization of man's various needs, material, intellectual,aesthetic and spiritual. These various needs, too, differ in quality and cannot be reduced to one, e.g., the material need, as is attempted by Marxian and neo-Marxian philosophy (Marcuse), so that all human values are quantified. These various needs exist side by side, each in its own right and being of equal importance. Man is balanced if he is able to give full and real expression to all these needs, thereby following his natural impulse in the particular situation in which he finds himself. It is then that he is a person or an individual in his own right, and it is by the very contradiction of his fellowman that he is confirmed as an individual. For it is by the experience of his own limitation in view of his being put in question by the other that he feels a self as against the self of the other. In short, it is the controversial relation, which holds between human visions of truth, or else the actual experience of the crisis in which he finds himself with the other, that causes him to feel himself as a self existing in a particular situation. It is thus obvious that the controversial relation separates man from his fellowman, but at the same time is man's very gateway to the other; for we have repeatedly shown that it is by this very relation that man and his fellowman are referred to each other.

We said that man is balanced if he is able to give expression to his various natural needs in a spontaneous way, as these needs arise in a particular existential situation. Man must thus be unbalanced if, by artificial construction, his natural needs, which differ from each other in quality, are reduced to one. That is to say, if either his material needs are regarded as secondary and are even deemed to be that from which man must free himself as much as possible in order to follow the dictates of reason, as was taught by Kant, Fichte and Hegel, for instance, or if his material needs are seen as basic and his other needs are all seen to be dictated by this need, as is taught by dialectical materialism, then man vanishes as a balanced person. He is absorbed either by Kant's moral law, by Fichte's transcendental ego, by Hegel's absolute spirit, or by the Marxian dialectical logos, i.e., the dialectical movement of history according to the objective laws of matter and economics.

But in the functionalistic approach of neo-positivist thought, too, man's material needs, in the sense of man's desire to improve his material well-being by gaining progressive control over the world through the functionalistic method, are really of primary concern. In the functionalistic approach, man's intellectual powers are all geared up to analytical activity in order to gain this end, even though, as Marcuse has pointed out, the social and political aims of neo-positivistic philosophy (the aim to retain the present monopolistic way of production but social structure of western society) are not immediately evident and hidden under the cloak of strict scientific neutrality. In the one-sided functionalistic approach, man's ethical, aesthetical and spiritual needs are denied their essentially different character and individual reality. By the descriptive method, they are functionalized as well and are treated as mere ways of speaking within the limits and according to the rules of certain language games. By linguistic analysis, therefore, the functionalistic method is able to draw a functional distinction between philosophical and ordinary common sense language, and, in so doing, stresses the value of the latter as being the vehicle of everyday life and the means of communication with regard to man's daily affairs.

In the existential approach, on the other hand, man's material needs and also, to some degree, his intellectual needs are neglected, and his ethical and spiritual needs for the irrational are emphasized. In the existential approach man, to speak with Jaspers, makes the jump into the transcendent, which he cannot grasp by his understanding, but which he experiences as the manifestation of being in his being-there (Heidegger), as a failure in the border-situation (Jaspers) and as the freedom of the nothing of his mind (Sartre). In all three cases, man creates himself from the nothing and in the midst of the nothing, by making a decision to be himself, a nothing, in the sense that he is temporal, periodical and finite. We have already observed how, by cutting himself loose from the world and by putting the emphasis on his being-there, he imposes a burden upon himself which is really superhuman and under which he must break up. Thus the one-sided nature and negative outlook upon life and the world of the existential vision of truth can only be overcome if the constitution of the world by man in the form of the various fields of culture and civilization, the sciences and technology, the humanities, the fine arts and theology, is realized to be man's permanent task, which he keeps performing in continual controversy with his fellowman. In other words, balance can only be restored if man's permanent activity in these fields is understood to be an act of self-realization, i.e., the gratification of man's different needs, material, intellectual, aesthetical and spiritual, and if the equal importance of these cultural fields of man's different vital needs is fully recognized.

Generally speaking, the history of philosophy teaches us the fundamental significance of the controversial relation that obtains between the human logoi. This controversial relation no longer presents itself as something negative, as something that must be overcome at all costs by the act of self-transcendence, i.e., the unilateral postulation as absolute of one particular philosophical alternative for coping with the crisis of truth. On the contrary, the permanent crisis-situation of our truths, or their constantly calling each other in question, reveals itself as something very positive, as the very motor of human culture and history. It shows itself as man's very bridge to his fellowman. The crisis is experienced by man and his fellowman as the *sufficient reason* and as the *real ground* of the human truth-perspectives, which, by the rational constitution of man's surroundings in conformity with his prevailing needs under particular circumstances, are aspects of the real. Last but not least, the crisis is the *ethical ground* of human truth; for it is by its actual experience that man and his fellowman are referred to one another in mutual self-control and self-restriction to their common field of action, in the spirit of tolerance, good will and humility. It is on the grounds of their common experience of the crisis that a real encounter takes place between them, that they really enter into communication with one another and that they are joined in real community of action. It is by the observation of their actual experience as their *empirical limit* that they obey the *moral ought*, and so lead an *authentic* or *ethical existence*, i.e., an existence in freedom from their own truth and their egocentricity.

If the philosophy of history has been recognized as man's mirror, i.e., as reflecting man's real nature as a historical and controversial being, then it may be said that it also discloses the real nature of philosophy as being historical and controversial. It would therefore be appropriate to describe philosophy as the *science of actuality;* for in its awareness of the empirical limit, as it is outlined by the controversial nature of human truth, philosophy becomes an empirical science of becoming, that is to say, it keeps itself open for the changing circumstances of life and changes its concepts accordingly. In other words, by assuming a self-critical attitude, philosophy will constitute and reconstitute the world in accordance with life's changing conditions. In so doing, it will, through controversy and debate among philosophers, provide man with new alternatives for coping with his current existential situation. The philosophical alternative that suits the situation best will be accepted by him as a temporary guide in the midst of conflict and uncertainty.

In order to enable man to lead a life in conformity with his real nature and thus an authentic existence, philosophy's task may be described as threefold. In the first place, this task is of a critical nature. That is to say, by pointing to man's empirical limit, as it has been described previously, philosophy should show the fallacy and folly of any kind of self-transcendence in an absolute manner. It should expose the dangers that lie in transcending man's empirical limit and in ignoring the actual experience of the crisis, no matter in what form such self-transcendence takes place, in a positive or in a negative form.

In the second place, philosophy, with reference to the prevailing circumstances of life and the particular human needs as they arise from the particular existential situation in which man happens to find himself, should make the attempt at formulating new concepts which answer this situation, but which lose their meaning as the conditions of life change. It should construct a new meaningful picture of the world in conformity with the latest achievements of the individual sciences and the humanities, a world-view that answers the need of the young generation for a new meaning of life and for new values, without leading them astray and raising false hopes in them, by dangling before their eyes the illusory picture of a *utopia* flowing with milk and honey. This is exactly what is being done by those who preach the cult of scientism as well as by those who tell the story of a universal historical logos of any kind whatsoever. The arduous belief in these utopian aims causes the young generation to forget man's limitation and to seek to convert the natural change by controversy into an absolute revolutionary change by force.

In the third place, philosophy should act as the guardian of *freedom*, and so as the guardian of a real community of men. In a view of man's empirical limit, to which the truth of the other clearly points, philosophy should summon man to act responsibly towards the other. That is to say, it should remind him of the obligation imposed upon him by the moral ought (which is implied by the empirical limit), namely, to respond positively to the other's challenge to compare notes and his claim to be heard. It is in this way that philosophy guides man to freedom, i.e., leads him to focus his attention upon his fellowman and, in creative cooperation with him, enter into a genuine community with him.

Man's everlasting concern about the authenticity of his existence, which reveals itself at present by the frustration and despair of the young generation, challenges philosophy to new self-reflection. The continually changing circumstances of life always cause the question of man's existence to be asked again. If philosophy aims at having a real content and wishes to avoid building castles in Spain or merely playing language games, it must take into account man's respective existential situation, which continually changes. It must realize that it, too, is subject to the moral ought that is implied by its empirical limit. By virtue of this, it must exercise self-restraint and, in the spirit of modesty and humility, must confine itself to the field of the actual crisis within which it operates. Philosophy can really be an empirical science only if it contents itself with remaining the science of man's actual contingent experience or, in this sense, the *science of actuality*. It must not make the attempt at absolute self-transcendence in any form whatsoever and so become total and dogmatic, but it must not try to reason itself away either and, in so doing, dissolve man and the the world into a set of functional relations or into a "set of pointer readings", as Sir Arthur Stanley Eddington so aptly put it. Let us remember that as long as man exists, so long will there be philosophy.

BIBLIOGRAPHY

S. Alexander, *Space, Time and Deity*, 2 vols., Macmillan, London, 1934[3].

J. L. Austin, *Philosophical Papers*, Clarendon Press, Oxford, 1961.

J. L. Austin, *Sense and Sensibililia*, Clarendon Press, Oxford, 1962.

A. J. Ayer, *The Foundations of Empirical Knowledge*, Macmillan, London, 1940.

E. Bernstein, *Evolutionary Socialism: A Criticism and Affirmation*, transl. by C. Harvey, Huebsch, N. Y., 1909.

E. Bloch, *Das Prinzip Hoffnung*, 3 vols., Suhrkamp, Frankfurt/M., 1967.

O. F. Bollnow, "Die menschliche Natur, ein Beitrag zur philosophischen Lage der Gegenwart", in: *Blätter für deutsche Philosophie*, XVI, 1942.

O. F. Bollnow, *Neue Geborgenheit (Das Problem einer Überwindung des Existentialismus)*, Kohlhammer, Stuttgart, 1955.

O. F. Bollnow, *Das Wesen der Stimmungen*, Klostermann, Frankfurt/M., 1956.

O. F. Bollnow, *Mensch und Raum*, Kohlhammer, Stuttgart, 1963.

O. F. Bollnow, *Existenzphilosophie*, Kohlhammer, Stuttgart, 1964[6].

O. F. Bollnow, *Französischer Existentialismus*, Kohlhammer, Stuttgart, 1965.

M. Born, *Von der Verantwortung des Naturwissenschaftlers*, Nymphenburger, Munich, 1965.

K. Breysig, *Die Meister der entwickelnden Geschichtsforschung*, De Gruyter, Berlin, 1936.

R. Carnap, "Die physikalische Sprache als Universalsprache der Wissenschaft", in: *Erkenntnis*, 2, 1932.

A. De Saint-Exupéry, *Citadelle*, Librairie Gallimard, Paris, 1958[2].

F. M. Dostoevsky, *Die Legende vom Grossinquisitor*, Furche, Hamburg, 1952.

M. A. Dynnik, M.T. Jowtschuk, B. M. Kedrow, M. B. Mitin, O. W. Trachtenberg, T. I. Oiserman, A. F. Okulow, *Geschichte der Philosophie*, 6 vols., Moscow, 1957, in German, V. E. B. Deutscher Verlag der Wissenschaften, Berlin, 1959.

F. Engels, "Introduction to Marx's Class Struggles in France", in: *K. Marx/F. Engels*, Selected Works in two volumes, vol. I, Berlin, 1960[10].

F. Engels, *Critique of the Social Democratic Draft Programme*, 1891, Sect. II.

F. Engels, *Herrn Eugen Dührings Umwälzung der Wissenschaft* (Anti-Dühring), Dietz, Berlin, 1960[13].

E. Gellner, *Words and Things*, Pelican Books, 1968.

B. Goldenberg, *Karl Marx, Ausgewählte Schriften*, Kindler, Munich, 1962.

E. Grisebach, *Gegenwart*, Niemeyer, Halle, 1928.

E. Grisebach, *Freiheit und Zucht*, Rascher, Zürich, 1936.

E. Grisebach, *Was ist Wahrheit in Wirklichkeit?*, Paul Haupt, Berne, 1941.

G. W. F. Hegel, "Der Endzweck" (des Geistes), in: *Hegel*, selected writings by F. Heer, Fischer, Frankfurt/M., 1955.

G. W. F. Hegel, "Die Politische Ordnung", in: *Hegel*, selected writings by F. Heer, Fischer, Frankfurt/M., 1955.

M. Heidegger, *Über den Humanismus*, Klostermann, Frankfurt/M., 1947.

M. Heidegger, *Erläuterungen zu Hölderlin's Dichtungen*, Klostermann, Frankfurt/M., 1951².

M. Heidegger, *Holzwege*. Klostermann, Frankfurt/M., 1952².

M. Heidegger, *Sein und Zeit*, Niemeyer, Tübingen, 1953⁷.

M. Heidegger, "Wer ist Nietzsches Zarathustra?", in: *Vorträge und Aufsätze*, Neske, Pfullingen, 1959².

M. Heidegger, "Was heisst Denken?", in: *Vorträge und Aufsätze*, 1959².

M. Heidegger, *Was ist Metaphysik?*, Klostermann, Frankfurt/M., 1960⁸.

F. H. Heinemann, *Existentialism and the modern Predicament*, Adam and Charles Black, London, 1958³.

W. Heisenberg, M. Born, E. Schrödinger, Pierre Auger, *On Modern Physics*, Orion Press, London, 1961.

F. Hoyle, *The Nature of the Universe*, Penguin, 1963.

F. Hoyle, *Frontiers of Astronomy*, Heinemann, London, 1955.

K. Jaspers, *Philosophie*, 3 vols., Springer, Berlin-Göttingen-Heidelberg, 1956³.

P. Keran, *La Confiance selon Otto Friedrich Bollnow (Un essai de dépassement de l'existentialisme)*, doctoral thesis submitted to the Faculty of Theology at the University of Strassbourg, 1966.

F. W. Konstantinow, *Grundlagen der marxistischen Philosophie*, Academy of the Sciences of the U. S. S. R. ,Moscow, in German, Dietz, Berlin, 1966.

G. Krüger, *Grundfragen der Philosopie*, Klostermann, Frankfurt/M., 1958.

R. C. Kwant, *De Fenomenologie van Merleau-Ponty*, Aula Boeken, Utrecht-Antwerp, 1962.

W. J. Lenin, Was tun?, in: *Werke*, vol. 5, Berlin, 1959³.

W. J. Lenin, "Der Imperialismus als höchtes Stadium des Kapitalismus", in: *Werke*, vol. 22, Berlin, 1960.

W. J. Lenin, "Staat und Revolution", in: *Werke*, vol. 25, Berlin, 1960.

W. J. Lenin, *Materialismus und Empiriokritizismus*, Dietz, Berlin, 1964.

H. Lipps, *Untersuchungen zu einer hermeneutischen Logik*, Klostermann, Frankfurt/M., 1959².

J. Locke, "On the Human Understanding", in: *The Works of John Locke*, Ward, Lock & Co., London.

K. Löwith, *Heidegger, Denker in dürftiger Zeit*, Fischer, Frankfurt/M., 1953.

G. Marcel, *Le Mystère de l'Etre*, 2 vols., Aubier (Editions Montaigne), Paris, 1963²

H. Marcuse, *Soviet Marxism*, Routledge & Kegan Paul, London, 1958.

H. Marcuse, *One-Dimensional Man*, Beacon Press, Boston, 1968⁵.

K. Marx, "Differenz der demokritischen und epikureischen Naturphilosophie", in: *K. Marx/F. Engels*, historico-critical complete edition, 1. section, vol. I, first half, Frankfurt/M., 1927.

K. Marx, "Speech at Amsterdam", 1872, quoted in Iu. M. Steklov, *History of the First International*, International Publishers, New York, 1928, p. 240.

K. Marx, "Konspekt der Debatten über das Sozialistengesetz", 1878, in: *Marx und Engels, Briefe an A. Bebel, W. Liebknecht, K. Kautsky, und Andere*, Verlagsgenossenschaft Ausländischer Arbeiter in der U. S. S. R., Moscow, 1933, p. 516.

K. Marx, "Das Elend der Philosophie", in: *K. Marx/F. Engels*, vol. 4, Berlin, 1959². In abridged form, cf. *Karl Marx, Ausgewählte Schriften*, ed. by B. Goldenberg, Kindler, Munich, 1962.

K. Marx, "Thesen über Feuerbach", in: *Karl Marx, Ausgewählte Schriften*, ed. by B. Goldenberg, Kindler, Munich, 1962.

K. Marx, "Manifest der Kommunistischen Partei", in: *Karl Marx, Ausgewählte Schriften*, ed. by B. Goldenberg, Kindler, Munich, 1962.

K. Marx, "Kritik der Hegelschen Dialektik und Philosophie überhaupt", in: *Karl Marx, Ausgewählte Schriften*, ed. by B. Goldenberg, Kindler, Munich, 1962

K. Marx, "Zur Kritik der Nationalökonomie", in: *Karl Marx, Ausgewählte Schriften*, ed. by B. Goldenberg, Kindler, Munich, 1962.

K. Marx, "Das Kapital", book III, abridged version, in: *Karl Marx, Ausgewählte Schriften*, ed. by B. Goldenberg, Kindler, Munich, 1962.

M. Planck, *Vom Relativen zum Absoluten*, Leipzig, 1925.

G. A. Rauche, *The Philosophy of Actuality*, Fort Hare University Press, 1963.

H. Reichenbach, *Wahrscheinlichkeitslehre*, 1935.

H. Reichenbach, *The Rise of Scientific Philosophy*, University of California Press, 1958.

F.-J. v. Rintelen, *Philosophie der Endlichkeit*, Hain, Meisenheim/Glan, 1960[2].

G. Ryle , *The Concept of Mind*, Hutchinson, London, 1949.

G. Ryle, *Dilemmas*, Cambridge University Press, 1954.

J.-P. Sartre, *Critique de la raison dialectique*, Librairie Gallimard, Paris, 1960.

A. Schaff, *Marx oder Sartre? Versuch einer Philosophie des Menschen*, Fischer, Frankfurt/M., 1966.

W. Schmiele, *J.-P. Sartre, Drei Essays*, Ullstein, Frankfurt/M., 1963.

E. Schrödinger, *Meine Weltansicht*, Fischer, Frankfurt/M., 1966.

W. Schulz, "Über den philosophiegeschichtlichen Ort Martin Heideggers", in: *Philosopische Rundschau*, 1,2,3,4,1953/54.

W. Schulz, *Der Gott der neuzeitlichen Metaphysik*, Neske, Pfullingen, 1957[3].

W. Schulz, *Wittgenstein, Die Negation der Philosophie*, Neske, Pfullingen,1967.

H. Spiegelberg, *The Phenomenological Movement*, 2 vols., Nijhoff, The Hague, 1960.

G. J. Warnock, *Berkeley*, Penguin, London, 1953.

L. Wittgenstein, *Tractatus Logico-Philosophicus*, Routledge & Kegan Paul, London, 1960[8].

L. Wittgenstein, *Philosophical Investigations*, Blackwell, Oxford, 1958.

DATE DUE